The Journey Within

A Memoir

Brenig Davies

New edition 2023

Published by
Llyfrau Cambria Books, Wales, United Kingdom.
Cambria Books is a division of
Cambria Publishing Ltd.
Discover our other books at: www.cambriabooks.co.uk

Reviews

"Searingly honest. Fascinating to learn about the author's life journey, the motor mechanic years, growing up in Aberfan, the choices he had to make - sometimes under considerable constraints, facing mental health challenges. A man who had a fulfilling career in education and was proud of what he achieved to meet the needs of vulnerable communities, an aim that was his primary intention throughout life. A very human memoir of a life well lived. Dedicated to service. Questions are raised about 'what is leftwing'? Absolutely riveting and accessible read".

Rhoda Thomas
Writer, poet, memoirist

"The whole book affirms the importance of education for the individual and for society: every school child, student and professional educator should read this book; it is an inspiration".

Ken Lever
Professor of telecommunications signal processing, Cardiff University, Retired

"A thoroughly engrossing memoir, that memorably captures the experience of what it is like to belong to but also to move away from a Valleys community with all the attendant feelings of rootlessness and loss of identity that this can bring. Interwoven with the narrative are a series of poignant reflections, which prompt the reader to think but which also tug at the heartstrings."

Ian Rees
Further Education College, Senior Manager

This book is written for and dedicated to my grandchildren
Anthony, Nancy, Luke, Gwenna, Ellie, Finley, Dylan, Arthur

Contents

Prologue

I have written this memoir to record the significant influences on my life. I have concentrated on my adult and working life but inevitably there is mention of my family and some commentary on where I was brought up.

Five influences have profoundly impacted the direction life has taken me: the particular nature of my home environment; the tragedy of the Aberfan disaster; my decision to move to London from the South Wales valleys and to work at Rolls Royce, my achievement of a First-Class Honours degree and subsequent career in the education sector, and a long undiagnosed mental health condition.

Throughout my life I have experienced exhilarating times, had a good deal of fun and, without wishing to seem immodest, feel I can be proud of my achievements. There have also, however, been difficult, disappointing, and worrisome times. From very early on, though my precise condition remained undiagnosed for a long time, I suffered from mental health issues. It is difficult to judge to what extent they may have affected my life choices, but I am pleased to say that now, as I write, at the age of seventy-eight, I am as happy and contended as I could wish.

2

1: Early Years

The only journey is the journey within

Rainer Maria Rilke

I was born in the village of Aberfan in South Wales in 1944 as World War Two was ending. Stories of the war form part of my earliest memories. I remember my maternal grandmother describing the sound of German aircraft returning to Germany having dropped their bombs on the docks of South Wales. Everyone then was highly patriotic, but I have always harboured a suspicion that unthinking patriotism borders too closely on nationalism, which can be dangerous, as we too readily see to this day.

The topography of South Wales is attractive, with its lush valleys and imposing sheer hilltops dramatically contrasting with the monolithic relics of the intensive heavy industry blighting the area. Sunny days, deep in the valley, are rarer than in the coastal belt of Cardiff directly south of the Taff valley and the weather will change dramatically with the seasons and even during the day.

In my village, and throughout the valleys, rows of terraced houses spread out from the pit – the colliery – where most men worked until the pit closed in the 1980s, shortly after the year-long miners' strike. The miners worked deep underground, cutting coal in narrow, low tunnels. It was hard, dangerous work, with not infrequent serious accidents and fatalities. In my childhood, the pit ambulance was parked opposite my home. It was dark blue with a bell to indicate an emergency. I would see the miners going to work and coming home in the evening while I was working in my first job serving petrol in the new garage of Aberfan.

Once a week, colliers would carry home a pack of wooden sticks to light their home coal fires. All employed in the pit would be given free coal and sticks. The coal would be delivered to each house in a coal lorry once a month; it would be carried to the 'coal house', at the back of the house, by those in the house who were strong enough to do so.

It was common to hear the coal miners coughing and spitting phlegm as they passed the garage. In later life, so many would die before their time of pneumoconiosis. Some miners would go straight to the pub or social club on their way home; many would drink *session beer*. *Session beer* is low in alcohol and cheap and a good way of rehydrating without being too hungover for work the next day.

University education or teacher training college was the way out for a few school leavers, but only a few people were able to pursue this avenue. When I served my five-year apprenticeship, the total number of young people going to university was around eight per cent. That was the figure for the whole of England and Wales. For children of families in the valleys it was much lower. Nowadays, the number of young people and adults beginning a degree is just below fifty per cent, and again slightly lower in poorer areas of the South Wales valleys. I draw attention to the notion of *beginning* a degree, because many students from the valleys will not complete their undergraduate studies, due to low peer and family support. The working-age population of the county boundary of Merthyr Tydfil, the town of the Taff valley, had and still has high rates of low educational qualifications, a disproportionately high benefit claimant rate and a declining middle class; in 2020 it figured amongst the poorest regions of the European Union.

Because of this, generations of families would remain in the pit village and still do, though the pit has long since gone, as mentioned above. It is an environment that encourages generations of family members to stay emotionally and physically close to one another. Proximity is a strong determinant of members sharing life and aspirations. It was what my parents wanted and expected of me. I knew, however, that remaining in Aberfan **wa**s not for me, though it was not until late adolescence that I became seriously inquisitive about living beyond the mountains of the Taff valley. I would look towards the mountains, from the garage where I was undertaking an apprenticeship, with competing emotions due to my sense of confinement and my determination to leave Aberfan. Though I had no idea where life would take me I knew I must leave the valley. Leaving when I did has had profound psychological consequences that remain to this day. When I visit my mother, who is 103 years old as I write, I occasionally meet former school friends who are not necessarily unhappy with their lives. It was just that moving out of Aberfan was a decision I knew I must take.

The psychological term for a family I grew up in is an *enmeshed* family, where emotions may fuse happily, or with some resignation, between family members. Enmeshment, to be maintained, needs to keep family members, which may comprise several generations, in a net which makes escape difficult. Parents often expect, or covertly demand, that their children provide unconditional support. They expect them to live nearby and adopt the family's beliefs and values.

Sometimes an enmeshed family needs a *black sheep* to reinforce family expectations; I was the family black sheep who left for London. It was shortly after the Aberfan disaster, when I was twenty-two, that I left to work for Rolls Royce. The psychological estrangement from the family is with me to this day, even with my mother at an advanced age. I feel gratitude to my parents for influencing my early years, but it is mixed with a sense that it was not their wish for me to escape the family. I believe that my independence of mind and the tenacity that I was fortunate enough to develop led to my good fortune in later life, however.

Along with all pupils in my junior school, I sat an examination at 11 years of age to determine who went to a grammar school and who went to a secondary modern school. Pupils who passed the 11+ examination went to grammar school and did academic subjects; pupils who failed the 11+ went to secondary modern school. Secondary modern schools were created after the Second World War, emphasising practical lessons, science, maths, and English. There were no final year examinations; schooling ended at 15. I failed the 11+ exam, with the consequent expectation that I would work not far from home. This is what my parents wanted and hoped for, and it became a self-fulfilling prophecy.

On completing the five-year apprenticeship, and after a short period in Merthyr bus garage, where I went to gain experience maintaining heavy vehicles, I moved to London to work for Rolls Royce as a mechanic. I was free of my enmeshed family. Four years later, I returned, married my long-term girlfriend, and had a temporary job teaching motor vehicle studies at Merthyr Tydfil College. Somewhere in the back of my mind I knew returning home was not an intelligent move. Nevertheless, I had gone from being a motor vehicle apprentice to teaching in an FE college within ten years. I felt good about my career, but not my return to Merthyr. I paid a heavy price returning to Merthyr years later. Education, I found, was my career *home*, though this only became evident four years later when I changed from teaching motor vehicle subjects to liberal education subjects.

Returning to Merthyr was not easy. I had left London behind; it had opened my mind to so much; new friends, new social, cultural and political experiences. I might have stayed had I accepted an offer to enrol on a teacher education course at Roehampton College, Southwest London. At that time, I was still working for Rolls Royce but now as a technician. I thought seriously about taking up the offer, but I was unsure if I had the intellect to cope with the demands of an academic course. Not leaping from an engineering career to an academic one plagued me for years. It was not helped by my parents refusing to help me financially through the course duration of one year, though my messing up the grant application didn't help.

I know now that taking the teacher education course would have pleased and stimulated me greatly, with all the reservations I had. My decision not to spend another year in London was strongly influenced by whether my fiancée would adjust to London life. It was a misplaced decision, though my education career did become successful years later. Further, there were practical considerations, such as if we could afford to live in the capital. These were all excuses perhaps to mask my lack of courage to begin married life in London.

On my final evening in London, I went for a drink with a fond friend, a friendship I wished for longingly. I mentioned to her that I was not looking forward to returning to Merthyr. My instincts lost out, though for many years my wife and I enjoyed a happy marriage with our two children. Then by late middle age, when our children had left home, we drifted apart and divorced, though it was not acrimonious, and we still have concern for each other.

I tried to recreate London life in Merthyr. Until we had our first child, my wife and I would go for a drink on the way home from work. That didn't work. The pubs were not full of people enjoying themselves, unlike London pubs. I thought Sunday lunchtime drinks in the Plymouth Arms in Saint Fagans, Cardiff, would be my London fix. It was not. We didn't know the people laughing with one another; they were of a different class, or so I thought.

While our children were growing up in Merthyr, I was determined to prepare the ground for them to go to university. I had achieved a first-class honours degree from University College, Cardiff, and later a Masters degree, both entirely through part-time study, with the help of my wife while bringing up two young children. I demonstrated that I could do much more with my increasing confidence and academic ability to progress my career in the further and higher education sectors. The failure of my 11+ examination was behind me, but it is possible that fear of failure and the consequences of failure early in life propelled me through episodes of adversity well into middle age.

2: Back to the Future

Roads? Where we're going we don't need roads!

Dr Emmett Brown (Doc) in 'Back to the Future'

So much has changed in my lifetime, although this is inevitable since I am currently seventy-eight years of age. The first man into space was in 1961. This was followed by the first man on the moon in 1969, the same year as the launch of the Open University. The prime minister described 1963 as a period of the 'white heat of technology'. Early main-frame computers were the size of large cabinets. Transport by passenger aircraft was mainly for the wealthy. Emigration to Australia by ship took over forty days. The first long-distance telephone call in the UK, a so-called trunk call, was made by the Queen in May 1958. A telephone operator connected all phone calls, usually made from a phone situated in people's hallways rather than from a living room or kitchen, and people answered in their *telephone voice*. Business accounts were recorded on hand-written ledgers. The terms laptop, iPad, iPhone and PC did not exist. It was a time before supermarkets and frozen foods. Longevity for those born the same year as me was 71 years for men and women. If born today, life expectancy for men is 75.5 years, and for women, 82.5 years, though it is lower in poor areas of the UK. The National Health Service was established four years after I was born. The concept of leisure time did not exist. The average hours worked per week in 1944 was 40 hours; it is now 32 hours. The number of vehicles on the roads in the UK in 1950 was four million; it is now over 39 million.

These innovations and many others have made life easier, safer and healthier in many ways. However, in some ways society has seen that some changes have produced deleterious effects and old practices have re-emerged to counter the damage caused by certain aspects of technological change.

There is increasing concern about the effects of global warming, which is considered to be the most serious issue facing the future of mankind. Motor vehicles are a significant contributor to unhealthy levels of air pollution. We know of the rush to produce motor vehicles that run on non-CO_2 fuels, such as electricity or hydrogen, though, of course, electricity and hydrogen may be produced by climate warming processes.

Filling up with petrol has changed. Self-service at petrol stations was introduced in the 1970s. Before that date, a petrol attendant would put petrol in for you. Checking tyre pressures was free. There were no automatic car-wash machines. Cars were washed by hand. Diesel was used in lorries, but not cars. It was a time with few cars in the village. Drink driving legal limits were introduced in 1967. A consequence was that driving some distance to a country pub became less attractive. Only now, concern about CO_2 emission is probably as much a factor as drink-driving laws when driving to a country pub, though I might be emphasising this a bit too much! It was a world without thought of climate change.

When I was young certain goods would be delivered to homes by horse drawn cart. I was fascinated watching the horse stop and start at each house without instruction from the delivery man; the horse would have learned the delivery route. The horse stopping and starting is certainly more efficient and more environmentally friendly than the stop-start motor vehicle. Throughout the route the horse would deposit dung on the road. If the dung was outside your house a shovel would quickly appear. It was sought after for garden manure that would decompose as fertiliser in order to be added to the garden vegetable patch!

I remember too, beer delivered to pubs in horse-drawn flat lorries called drays, with wooden beer barrels. Beer was brewed with natural ingredients, free of chemicals. Beer would not be delivered over long distances, especially over rough roads from the brewery, otherwise its condition would be affected, and it might lose its original taste. To overcome the travel limitation, each town and some large villages would have breweries not too far from pubs. It was not uncommon for draymen to get free beer from customers and their employers - 10 to 14 quarts (11 to 16 litres) a day.

Nowadays, beer without chemicals is called craft beer, but somehow or other, the beer manages to travel long distances. Perhaps this is due to better roads and better lorry suspensions.

Few houses had indoor lavatories, or *lavs* as we called them. Outside toilets did not have lift-up seats. The seat was made of wood over a round hole. Once the necessary business was completed, waste would be flushed away by pulling a chain from the water tank above the *lav* seat. Mothers could be heard shouting to their child, "Have you pulled the chain?".

Terraced houses where manual workers lived were unlikely to have bathrooms. Body washing was in a small room with just a basin, called a bosh. The expression for washing this way was 'having a swill in the bosh'; the expression is still used by some these days when taking a quick upper-body wash. A bosh is a large porcelain tank, which was used in ironworks where men would have a good swill at the end of their working day. Colliers would take a complete body wash once a week in a tin bath placed in front of the living room coal fire. Hot water was heated on the iron hearth of the coal fireplace. Once dried off, the collier would always put on clean underpants to last a week.

There were coal fires in most rooms. It was the time before radiators and central heating. It was commonplace for women to stand with their back to the coal fire and raise their skirt – from the back!

Pit-head baths, with showers, were introduced in collieries in the early 1950s. Colliers would shower on finishing their daily work shift before going home. Showers replaced the weekly tin bath. Where there was space, a spare room was turned into a bathroom; or often, a bathroom would be added as an extension to the house. It is fascinating to recognise these days that water is considered and managed as a scarce resource. The convenience of flowing water at the turn of a tap was taken for granted without any concern about limiting water use. However, there might be only one tap, usually in the kitchen. 1990 marked the start of widespread use of domestic water metering.

It was still the time of a few steam-driven vehicles. Aberfan had one of the remaining steam-driven road-rollers. It was designed to be very heavy, with large wide stone wheels to damp down the road surface. The driver of the village stream roller was huge and very fat with it. It was not until years later that it dawned on me that the large and fat driver was not a deliberate ploy to make the steamroller even heavier!

Clothes were more environmentally friendly than today. I had one of everything: one pair of best shoes; one pair of daps – called plimsolls in middle-class neighbourhoods of Cardiff - one suit; one warm raincoat; woollen underpants; body vests and swimming trunks that had a most dangerous tendency to come down to my ankles when wet, and two pairs of socks made of wool. Socks would not wear well but they would have an extended life by darning, usually heel and toes. Darning is knitting with wool the worn out part of a sock. The concept of 'climate miles' did not exist because so much was made or grown locally or somewhere in Britain. People wore clothes until they couldn't anymore. It was not unusual to see a man gardening in his old suit. There was no such thing as leisurewear because there was so little time for leisure. Men and women were too tired to do many physical leisure activities when they came home from work. Manual workers would go to bed on a Sunday afternoon for a nap; my father did. The health benefit of a nap is acknowledged these days.

There would be no knitting on Sunday in my home, on religious grounds. Clothes were knitted – jumpers, cardigans, men's underpants. Knitting clothes was a necessity. Nowadays, there is still knitting, often as a pastime, perhaps in knitting groups. Knitting has replaced darning socks and become a mental health therapy.

A phenomenon which might surprise today's generation was the annual appearance of the Sioni Winwns (Jonnie Onions) man from Brittany wearing traditional Breton clothes. The Sioni Onions man would go from house to house on his bicycle selling his distinctive pink onions, a string of which would be strung around his body. Breton onions are now bought from supermarkets. No longer is the Breton man to be seen with his bike, black beret, and navy blue and white jumper with twenty-one stripes. Breton jumpers have stripes so I have learned, because fishermen and sailors off the Brittany coast would be easier to spot if they fell overboard. I will say more about my own penchant for the Breton jumper in Chapter 15.

Gardening provides a perfect example of the way in which we have

11

realised that some of the activities and processes that we thought were outdated have been revisited. My memory is that the whole area of a typical garden would be used for the cultivation of fruit and vegetables, but no chemicals were used to enhance growth of garden produce. Who would have thought that this absence of chemicals would one day be reinstated and rebranded as organic food? Soil in the South Wales valleys is black due to the coal outcrop near to the surface; in contrast, the soil south towards the coastal belt is a rich dark brown.

I first saw the difference when I would go to the Vale of Glamorgan for a ride in the car with my parents. I was fascinated by the change in the colour of the soil. To me it was a dramatic early sign of the wealth in the Vale of Glamorgan, compared with coalfield valley communities.

Funerals were events to respect. Men would doff their caps and stop at the side of the road until the cortège had passed. Curtains would be drawn closed in the family home of the deceased. In the valleys, there were no funeral homes. The body, in a coffin, would be laid in the front room, often called the best room or parlour.

The Merthyr valley was a football valley with the town football team having a greater following than rugby. Merthyr rugby club never did succeed in attracting large crowds and developing into a top-tier club; largely, I believe, due to the team's coaches, most of whom were schoolteachers. Even in an overwhelmingly working-class town, being a prominent rugby club member offered low middle-class preferment. Merthyr rugby club members guarded their elite practices, even though it was not an elite Welsh club. There is an instance that I personally know of where a local professional football player entered the club with a rugby friend, but no interest was shown in him, despite his successful football career.

Merthyr football team was successful in the lower English leagues. The club and its supporters were essentially working-class and unpretentious. I would wait eagerly for my father to return home from the match by looking out for the football bus; to hear the score would excite me greatly, especially if Merthyr Town won!

Transport demonstrates how we have realised that all change is not progress. Use of public transport, rather than everyone using their own car, is now viewed as a good thing. When I was a child, Cardiff still had trams. Trams are now reappearing in major cities of the UK. Electrically powered trolley buses replaced trams. Also, electrically powered buses are being introduced in several major cities. My father would go to work by a special bus. Buses would take colliers to the Pit. Factories had their scheduled buses. As children we would play football, and it would be football not rugby, on the main road, but we would look out for factory buses which might stop play. Trains would take day-trippers to the seaside. Once a year, town and village chapels, churches, including evangelicals, would join to organise a special charter day-trip train to Barry Island. British Rail would always meet Jehovah's Witnesses' request that the type of carriage would enable them to walk along the train knocking at each compartment to proselytise, or so it is said.

Once our chapel parishioners had formed a group on the beach, we as children would dash to the ice cream parlour for the biggest annual treat of all – a knickerbocker glory. Some sixty years later, now living in Barry, I went to buy a knickerbocker glory; to my great disappointment, the ice cream parlour had gone, and so had the knickerbocker glory. The other childhood thrill was to buy a water pistol; but, of course, one can still buy these.

When I was a school pupil, the blackboard – now called a chalkboard because of sensitivities toward the word *black* – and white chalk was mainly the only teaching aid. Coloured chalk came later; teachers were excited by new boxes of coloured chalk. The chalkboard has been replaced as a teaching aid by electronic white boards now, of course.

One memory I have of those times concerns the police. At the time, 'bobbies on the beat' were commonplace; almost without exception there would be village police stations with a sergeant and several policemen. While I was growing up the police had a special status or, more to the point, a status they dare not have today. It was not so much a special status but more that they had special 'privileges' which were taken for granted then but that would cause severe disciplinary action today. There were practices that could lead to a policeman being compromised, such as receiving produce from certain shops. Also, many policemen would not be charged for a bus journey. Just as seriously, and certainly much more dangerous, on the evening of the annual police ball, the police would drive home with impunity, despite having consumed well over a safe level of alcohol. In fact the legal limit of driving with alcohol in the blood did not become law until 1967.

Until the early 1960s, the 'knife man' would come around about twice a year. Kitchen utensils were expensive after the war due to a shortage of steel because a great deal had been used in armament production. Also, what steel there was, was of poor quality. Unlike nowadays, where so much is ready sliced, knives were used more, and consequently, they would become blunt and difficult to use. Knives were also, comparatively, much more expensive in those days. The 'knife man' would travel from village to village with a foot-driven stone wheel and sharpen the blunted knives to extend their life. This was done for a small charge.

The city of Sheffield was famous for the quality of its steel and metal implements for the home. Like many of today's products, not much cutlery is made in the UK; it is mainly sourced from Asian countries. This example of failing to manufacture products for our home market has not helped the UK's economy. The low cost of producing all kinds of products is not as attractive as it seems in a time of deep concern for greenhouse gases. Products manufactured in Asia are transported in ever-increasingly large freight ships, which expel dangerously high levels of CO_2. It is another example of where there ought to be a *back to the future* technology with more products made in the UK.

Another interesting example, though it might seem insignificant, of the way in which change can be seen as cyclical rather than linear is the sweeping up of garden leaves. Over the last few years there has been increasing use of garden blowers powered by petrol or electricity. These CO_2 producing machines have replaced the zero CO_2 product called a brush! The same applies to road sweeping. Men employed by the local authority would keep the streets clean with cane brushes, but of course there was little litter in days gone by. Today the cane brush has been replaced by mechanical vehicles for road sweeping.

Prior to today's plethora of national and local radio stations there was the BBC Home Service and the Light Programme, and later the Third Programme, which was launched on 29th September 1946. The Home Service was an early Radio 4; the Light Programme an early Radio 2. A popular show on the Light Programme was 'Music While You Work', listened to by millions of factory workers during the working day, playing popular music; it ended when Radio1 began in 1967. I still remember the Light Programme for its comedy programmes. They were not to be missed. Some of the comedy programmes would not be allowed on the radio today due to their non-PC remarks since adherence to political correctness is prominent in the BBC handbook for producers; recently confirmed as the BBC woke book, I'm told.

One such comedy programme was 'The Archie Andrews Show'. There was only one comedian on the programme, or two if you count the ventriloquist's dummy. It beggars belief now but the programme starred a ventriloquist's dummy 'Archie Andrews' used by ventriloquist Peter Brough on the radio!

Gay meant being happy, not a homosexual. That a manly man might be a homosexual was unknown to me. Lesbianism was not part of my vocabulary. Racism for me, and I was not alone, did not exist as a concept or word; but, of course, it did as a negative attitude. The term mixed-race did not exist, certainly not as a PC description. An older woman in Aberfan was called Flory Darkie; no offence was meant or taken by Flory. She was mixed-race. Lamentably the notions of equal opportunities and disability were not widely addressed. Disabled persons were hidden from view.

3: Growing Up

Always bear in mind that your own resolution to succeed is more important than any other one thing

Abraham Lincoln

At junior school I felt invisible in the classroom. The only thing I do remember, at the age of five, is that my teacher, Mrs Williams, mentioned to my mother that I was a nice boy and polite. Being a nice polite boy was not a welcome personal characteristic when I wanted to be seen as an ordinary boy. For the best of reasons, my parents treated me as being special, with the consequence that there were times when I was ill-equipped for mixing easily with my friends. Nevertheless, my childhood was a happy one. It is just that unpleasant experiences seem more readily to sear one's mind.

There is one other significant memory of junior school. I was about seven when the teacher, Mr Evans, in a maths lesson, asked me to sit at the front, facing the class. He placed the arithmetic sum in front of me on the desk and asked me to tell the class the answer. A dazzling shaft of sunlight was beaming through the window, making it impossible to read the calculation; it was made worse with me being nervous in front of the class. I knew I would not get the correct answer; the paper was a blur. The teacher laughed and ridiculed me in front of the whole class.

There are two traumatic athletic events that I think about uneasily from time to time. The first occurred after I had joined a boys' club in the next village to Aberfan. I took part one evening in a four-mile race for which I had not trained. Early into the road race anxiety set in, affecting my breathing. I had to stop running and walk back through the village to the boys' club feeling absolute humiliation. The second relates to my setting the school record for the hop-skip and jump (now called the triple jump). Without my knowing, the secondary school physical education teacher had entered me for a regional athletic event in Cardiff. I went down by bus on my own, with the journey taking about an hour. I arrived at the stadium with no idea what to do to participate in the event. Where in the stadium field should I go to register? With whom should I speak for guidance? What time was my event? My confusion led to flight, and I caught the bus home.

Returning home from school could be fun. Street games would come around regularly at times in the year. One game I remember is marbles. It might take us ages to get home, but parents would not be worried in those days. The game of marbles involved flicking small, coloured glass balls in the roadside gutter. It was safe to play in the gutter, with little traffic in those days, but tragedy can strike at a moment's notice. I was ten years of age when one of my friends was killed. A group of friends had been playing with him earlier in the day. He was on his way home through his back garden gate. As he closed the garden gate, a stone plinth fell on him. I can't remember how we learned of the accident. What I do remember is an absolute emptiness that a friend was no more. The street was quiet. His father owned a man's clothes shop in Merthyr; passing the shop was a constant reminder.

One good friend lived alongside the river Taff. His mother had a general store attached to the long terrace of houses built for miners by the colliery owners; it was a form of today's social housing. In the summer school holidays we would spend days boating on the river in a boat we had made ourselves. Higher up the river we would play *hit the French letter* (*French letters* are condoms if you are under 45 years of age!) in the *sewerage farm* by aiming stones at them as they floated by. There were two houses close to the sewerage farm for *sewerage families*. To this day they are known as the *sewerage semis*! We would camp on the steep mountainside for days with a methylated spirit camping cooker and an ample supply of baked beans. Our parents would not be unduly concerned for our safety.

Train-spotting was popular when I was young. I would follow this hobby with an older friend, who lived opposite my home; in fact he was the son of the schoolteacher who had ridiculed me in the maths lesson. We would go by train to Cardiff General Station (now Cardiff Central) and change platform at the station to where the express trains to London and other major cities would be standing. Steam engines pulled the trains. They were huge with a wonderful smell of oil and steam. It was a boy's dream to be a train driver. I would be in awe in the proximity of an express train with smoke billowing out of funnels. Even now, when I walk into a college engineering workshop, I enjoy the scent of oil; it takes me back to my time as an apprentice motor mechanic.

The purpose of train-spotting is to see and note the engine's number and put a line through the Ian Allan train-spotting book for the region. In much of South Wales the train services would be the Great Western Railway. The regions kept the names of the train companies prior to nationalisation of rail services in 1948. The nationalised railways became British Rail until 1994, when they were returned to private ownership. One of the most famous companies was Virgin Rail, owned by the entrepreneur Richard Branson; it was he who conceived the marketing brand Virgin, first used for Virgin mail-order record retailing.

On the closing of the Merthyr to Cardiff railway going through Aberfan, the nearest railway station was on the other side of the river Taff, in Merthyr Vale. The station would have an office for each track. One office would be the ticket office. In winter, the station office would be warmed by a coal fire. Many people smoked cigarettes and would do so while waiting for the train. As the train arrived, the cigarette would be stamped out with a foot. To ensure it was no longer smoking, the foot would be twisted with great skill. Notwithstanding the length of the cigarette, it would mostly be stamped on before leaving the ticket office. Cigarettes were much cheaper then; this was, in part, due to lower taxation. When I was young, cigarette smoking was not considered a danger to health; therefore, taxation was not used as a strong deterrent. The ticket office would offer rich pickings for partially smoked cigarettes, known as fag-ends or nips. The fag-ends provided a free nicotine kick for some. We would watch men – I can't remember women – picking up the half-used cigarettes for a short smoke (called a drag) out of sight of others. The half-used *nips* were highly valued.

Aberfan had two streets where the poor lived. One street, a row of houses overlooking the pit, was called *dog and tub*. The whole terrace had the appearance of coal dust from the colliery. My memory is a bit hazy, but as I remember, the children living there always seemed dirty, unkempt, and clad in ragged clothes.

It was an area to be avoided, though not because it was rough, it was more its reputation of uncleanliness. We didn't know the children; they went to a different primary school, but to the same secondary school. I can't remember them being dressed any differently from my friends in secondary school, and their behaviour was the same as the rest of the class. What I do remember of some boys from *dog and tub* is them swimming in the river Taff, in the summer. My friends and I would watch them from a road bridge as they dived into the river, careless of the river being full of colliery waste and over-spill from the many factories up-river in Merthyr. One factory made products using heavy chemicals. Today the river is clean, populated by salmon and trout. Salmon are spawning in the upper reaches of the Taff for the first time in 200 years, says the South East Wales Rivers Trust.

The bridge over the river Taff provides a good example of how essentially working-class the village of Aberfan was. I'm not sure of the date, but sometime in the 1960s a double decker bus overturned into the river, making the bridge unsafe for heavy vehicles and buses a while later; this resulted in a hitherto convenient bus route being rerouted. It was until 2013 that a new bridge was built north of Aberfan. However, this has resulted in the doubling of the traffic through the main road of Aberfan, where my mother lives. That it took such a long time to reroute the road confirms the lack of political leverage of Aberfan residents. I doubt very much that the delay of building a new bridge and in a location with negative consequences of the increase in traffic would have been tolerated by a middle-class community.

Along with all children at twelve years of age who failed the 11+ examination, I would continue my education in a secondary modern school. The name of the school reveals its status: it was *secondary* in terms of status certainly. The term 'modern' was unfortunate, however, for the curriculum was anything but modern. In the local education authority of Merthyr Tydfil secondary modern schools were different from grammar schools in two respects: Grammar schools had a uniform policy. Secondary schools did not.

The curriculum in grammar schools was based on academic subjects. In secondary modern schools the curriculum was biased towards practical subjects.

Pupils in grammar school would take examinations in academic subjects at fifteen years of age, and at seventeen years of age if they stayed in school for two years beyond compulsory education. There were no examinations in secondary modern schools, when all children finished their schooling at fifteen years of age.

Boys wore long trousers in grammar school from form one. In my secondary modern school, it was in Year Two that boys voluntarily began to wear long trousers, except me. I was the last boy in Year Two who was still wearing short trousers. It was my mother's choice. I pleaded with her to buy me long trousers like the other boys. Why should I be the only one with freezing legs? Inuits are protected from the cold, why shouldn't I? Short or long: it was more to do with a temperature below 0 degree Celsius on many winter days in the valleys and not manhood desperately calling. The issue of short trousers would not have arisen if the secondary school had had a uniform policy. Uniforms in my mind, then and now, are a public statement of pride, the collective association of success, unlike the dark side of failure for a secondary modern school pupil.

Secondary school was not a particularly happy time, though there were periods of fun. I can't remember anyone fully enjoying school, except for sport, and getting *out* of the open-air swimming pool in the middle of winter. No swimming lessons, just a cold shock!

While I was in the 'A' group, lessons were often seemingly pointless with no choice of subjects, and they were certainly not **modern**, whatever modern was meant to be. I know now that the curriculum was dated and not challenging; with no homework or marked class work, or examinations. I was an average pupil. It was only in athletics that I was better than most. To my amazement, I was exceptionally skilled at catching the ball in cricket. I always came second in the 100 yards sprint. No matter how much I tried, and did I try, I was always second, and always pipped at the finishing line by a friend. I was in the football team playing right-wing owing to my speed, occasionally controlling the ball! It was the age before *subs* (replacement player). The subs would be the reserves only if a player broke his leg! Thankfully, I escaped breaking a leg or being a reserve. The football was the old leather type that would get heavy when wet. There were two football pitches in Aberfan. One was laid on the spoils of the pit, and the playing service was hard with little grass. This pitch was fast in all weather conditions and suited my physique. The other pitch was laid as a football pitch with grass and a reasonable playing surface. When wet the ball was so heavy, I had difficulty kicking it over a reasonable distance to other team players. There was one occasion when my father came to see me playing in the rain. I could feel his sadness that my footballing skill and strength fell well short of what he hoped for his son. Nevertheless, my interest in playing football continued beyond my school days, though my interest was much greater than my skill. For one away game, playing for Treharris Boys Club, against Ynysybwl Boys Club, I captained the under 15s team. The other side didn't know I was 16!

I've mentioned that I was a well-behaved pupil. Though one day it was with much surprise that, apparently, I did something wrong. I've no idea of my wrongdoing, but I do remember the penalty. Corporal punishment was a whack by a cane delivered by a teacher across the palm of your hand. The PT teacher had exercised his power over a boy of thirteen. The same teacher would instruct the boys to sit on the top rung of wooden bars in the school gym. I learned the meaning of vertigo years later; I was terrified, and I was not alone in my trepidation. It's interesting that PT teachers were later renamed PE (Physical Education) teachers, to emphasise that there was education involved, rather than mere drill. Later again the term 'Sports Science' was introduced, to give the subject increased status. Halfway through secondary schooling, a fresh subject was introduced by a new teacher. Politics and Social Studies was a dream come true, and I could relate to the topics. There was discussion in each lesson. Teaching was not didactic. We were encouraged to give our views. I began to feel

21

confident; it seemed like a new school. But the old school still existed.

Members of Merthyr's Labour Party, who controlled the local education authority, were as ignorant as they were proud of their grammar school's sports policy. Never was this ignorance so painfully manifest as in the distinctions made between rugby and football. Secondary Modern schoolboys played only football; Grammar schoolboys played football *and* rugby. This amounted to the social apartheid of sport, and inverted snobbery. Football was a working-class game. First class rugby clubs and international teams attracted a higher social status than football, with occupational preferment in the public sector for some outstanding rugby players. When the first comprehensive secondary school opened in Troed-y-Rhiw, (Merthyr) in 1967, rugby and football were both on the curriculum, with the immediate end to sport apartheid. The game of rugby is popularly said to be the game of Wales, and it is, but while international rugby games attract crowds in the thousands, professional football games attract large crowds week-in-week-out, whereas club rugby matches attract gates of only a few hundred in many cases.

During my four years in secondary modern school, I worked as a shop delivery boy with a shop bike. There was one delivery I did once a week to a farm on the hillside. It was my penultimate delivery one particular day. It was so hard to push the shop bike up to the farm that I left the bike, with the last delivery of groceries, some distance below the farm. To my horror, when I returned to deliver the final order, it was to find that sheep had eaten the groceries. There was only one thing to do: go home, and not tell the shop owner. A few hours later, the shop owner came to my home to ask why I hadn't delivered the last order. There my job as delivery boy ended.

During the school holidays, I would occasionally help my uncle and aunt deliver fresh bread in their bread van. My uncle would be in his bakehouse very early each morning baking bread for delivery the same day; it was a hard life. I became hungry one day. I know what to do, I thought, I would take a little bit of crust off each loaf of bread, so my uncle and aunt would not notice it. By the end of the day my aunt and uncle had found me out. My aunt made my mother pay for every loaf from which I had taken a piece. My parents were undisturbed by my actions, but they were disturbed that my mother's sister had made her pay for the nibbled bread.

Holidays were limited to local journeys due to my father's thrombotic leg. We went to Mumbles, and Llansteffan, in West Wales, where we picked cockles and laverbread. Smoked bacon, fried egg with cockles and laverbread on toast is a traditional Welsh breakfast. Laverbread is known colloquially as Welsh caviar. Porthcawl, we went to twice and stayed in digs - breakfast and evening meal; it was commonplace at the time. At the end of the week, I would be bought a Dinky toy model car that I had been eagerly looking at all week. We also had a short visit to Burnham-on-sea, Essex, to visit former neighbours. I had two holidays in Weston-Super-Mare, taken by my parents' friends due to my father's illness. We travelled to Weston by paddle steamer from Cardiff. Weston had an attractive Winter Garden. The term and concept of a *winter garden* I could not comprehend; it would blow my mind. We would not miss going to chapel on Sunday, even on holiday; it was there that I learned to be embarrassed. My parents' friends would deliberately sing hymns louder than anyone else in the congregation. Pews provided no hiding place to relieve embarrassment.

My first holiday with my girlfriend and two friends was to the Spanish resort of Pineda de Mar. It was just becoming a package holiday resort and was not much more than a fishing village. There were few hotels, with fewer English pubs. We flew from Cardiff airport in a Dakota aircraft. Dakota aircraft were surplus to World War Two. These and other aircraft bought by entrepreneurs promoted the rapid growth in foreign holidays.

On the holiday we had a pointless quarrel with our friends. It is an example of how irritatingly quarrelsome I was when I was young. I'd like to believe that this quarrelsome period of my life was good practice for my ability to persuade in later life, especially as I became senior in my education career, but perhaps not. But I think closer to the truth, in early adulthood I became a total bore with some of my friends, as I was forever arguing on party politics and social issues. In today's language I was a complete woke.

Later, married with two children, a boy and a girl with two years between them, my wife and I holidayed for years in static caravans in France. Money was always tight, and we usually only just made it there and back in cars that didn't like French roads. As time went by, we could afford a more reliable car, but buying a car on credit stretched our budget somewhat, so we bought several tents and holidayed in the UK in the long summer holidays I enjoyed because I was a teacher. We had a Mini that was clearly too small to take a tent, so I made a trailer. I say more about my cars in Chapter 15. The tent allowed us to escape at weekends from the first house we bought, and one that we should never have bought.

It was a house in a good part of town, but unbeknown to us, it was on the route from the town pubs to a large housing estate. We were frequently kept awake on weekends by groups making their way home kicking empty beer cans. For this and other reasons we put the house up for sale.

As a teenager, Sundays in South Wales were awful; they were boring in the extreme. All shops and places of entertainment were closed, and it always seemed to rain. I have memories of drizzle, which is much worse than heavy rain, and an expectation that I must go to chapel; not once, but morning, afternoon, and evening – three services in one day. There would be frequent uncontrollable outbursts of giggling as we sat in the pews upstairs. However, we did try our best to listen to the preacher, with his homilies of world-class length. It was painfully boring for one long hour and more. Aching buttocks from sitting on hard wooden pews is my lasting memory of a preacher's sermon. Elderly deacons were spared aching buttocks as they sat on worn and dirty tapestry cushions in their reserved pews in the front row close to the pulpit. I assumed they sat in the front row so they could hear the preacher, but now I'm beginning to think it was to save their worn-out rumps after a life of manual work in the pit as colliers. I should have been more sympathetic to their aching bones and more respectful of their deacon status.

The preacher would conduct services mornings and evenings.

Either side of the sermon would be hymns, two prayers, and a reading by a parishioner. Occasionally there would be a guest preacher from another English Baptist chapel. The guest preacher assumed that the congregation expected a more profound and lengthy sermon, and he never disappointed – well at least with length! It became impossible to know when he, and always he, would end. For sure, a Swiss stopwatch, with an alarm, would have a fair chance of him keeping close to the hour. It never happened. On one occasion, the preacher had a cut on his face, obviously, from shaving. Giggles reached a noise just short of 60db when a friend whispered, 'Better if he cut the sermon, not his face'.

Morning sermons were lighter than the evening. The afternoon was called Sunday school and was usually led by a deacon of the chapel in the vestry. Something close to Christian fairy stories filled the hour. Ten adolescents would be considered a full house. The *fairy stories* confirmed that deacons had long since forgotten their adolescent emotions and urges.

For the morning service we sat in the upstairs row directly to the right of the pulpit, facing the sparse, predominantly female, congregation, all of whom would be wearing hats. In turn each of us would read a verse from the Bible New Testament. The verses were on something the size of two postage stamps with an image from the Bible. I often wonder if speaking every Sunday morning prepared me, a little, for public speaking in my subsequent career in education.

My mother insisted that I wear a suit and walk to the English Baptist chapel with my sister, who is five years older than me. I would be terrified that my friends would see me with my sister, for most of them did not go to chapel. Few of my friends had a suit, while I had a suit, white shirt, and tie with brown highly polished shoes. My father insisted that my shoes were clean; I think it was because of his time working in a shoe shop in Aberdare. It was the wrong apparel for a puny boy desperately rushing, yet struggling, to manhood. Curly hair didn't help either, with parishioners reminding my mother how lucky she was that I had bubbly curly hair. It did little to boost my confidence, and I was desperately trying to manage all the tricks adolescence plays on physique, face, personality, relationships and emotions with both my peers and my parents.

I was fifteen, and apparently a Christian. It was easier than being agnostic. It was easier than being an atheist. Now at seventy-eight I'd rather settle for humanism. Really, I'm uninterested in all categories, but there is a spiritual side to me. To play safe with my Baptist friends, I *stayed* a Christian. To be a Christian outrider I found to be comfortably disingenuous, but what the hell. I was at ease staying with the small herd of Christian friends who did seem to believe in God. It was not the time or place to hone my polemical skills, with God close by. I would keep my political argumentative skills for later in life. I did not want to exercise my non-beliefs. I stayed with being a Christian for peace of mind and remaining with a wonderful group of friends.

Sunday came every week. Sunday afternoon came every week. It was worse than secondary school. But this Sunday was special; I was to be baptised. The tiled pool of cold water –*cold* water, which was something to do with penitence, so I thought – was underneath the pulpit. In white gowns, hiding jeans, we were laterally dipped in the pool. I was baptised! I felt the same late afternoon as I did early afternoon, and still did not believe in God, but I was still a respectable member of my group of friends. We shared our piety, that's what friends are for!

Before I put religion to rest, my son, when he was six, asked if there was a God. I answered that if you believe in God then there is a God. End of.

Saturday was much more exciting with my two friends. Hot pie in the village Italian café. Heated meat pie, heated by inserting the steam metal pipe of the coffee machine, with brown sauce a penny extra, finished off with a mug of hot chocolate. We had a meal independent of our parents – we were growing up but not straying from the village. For me, and only me, straying from the village would come later when I went to London to work for Rolls Royce; I was twenty-two.

The piety would not hold the group for long. Friendships drifted; most went to teacher training college, either in Swansea or in Cardiff. I stayed home as an apprentice motor mechanic in Aberfan. My choice to become an apprentice and not become a clerk, working for British

Rail at Pontypridd station, as my mother wanted, was a significant gamble in testing the boundary of my status in an enmeshed family.

My mother wanted me to wear a white shirt and tie to work in a clean office in Pontypridd railway station. (The station was the longest island platform in the World when built in 1907.)

Becoming an apprentice motor mechanic wearing overalls was not an occupation befitting my parents' emerging middle-class status, though they didn't know they were almost middle class. My father still read *The Daily Mirror*. Later in life, I persuaded him to take *The Western Mail*, but that wasn't long-lasting; *The Daily Mirror* soon reappeared. Yet my father was intelligent, though not well educated. He left school one year earlier than his two siblings owing to his mother being unable to keep the three in school. He had the prerequisite skills to flourish in education. His handwriting was perfectly formed and composed with sophisticated language and had a gift for mental arithmetic.

A sign that you are moving towards the end of your teenage years is when you begin to look further afield for social enjoyment. In my case, it was going to the cinema, first by bus, and then dancing, usually by car. Dance venues were different from the nightclubs of today.

Almost every village had a cinema, and towns would have several cinemas. A visit to the cinema was different then. There were two films, one called the *main* film, and a shorter film called the B film; the B film came first! The logic would be to call the first film the A film and then the B film, but there we are. Between the B film and the main film, there would be Pathé News, in black and white, for about ten minutes. In the short break between the two films, ice-cream, sweets, chocolates and cigarettes would be served on a special tray by usherettes at the front of the theatre. Pathé News provided brief coverage of UK and international news, which at times dealt with wars. I remember news of the Korean War vividly and slightly nervously; it would worry me as I went to bed. I suffered the same worried emotion having seen news of the US Vietnam war at home on television. Many cinemagoers would look forward to Pathé News as it was the primary form of visual news.

It was the early days of television, which was provided by BBC., programmes were for a couple of hours each evening. Few homes had a television set. We did not have a television for some time, but we were one of the first in Aberfan. Several months before that, my father took me to his friend's house many miles away to view television for the first time. The programme was *Andy Pandy*; very popular with pre-school children, but I was not a young child! Television screens were not flat but slightly curved like a large light bulb; they called the curved screen a tube. Interestingly, curved TV screens these days are high-end televisions. I was fascinated with images on the screen and can remember trying to look around the screen to see if I could see Andy Pandy coming onto the screen, rather like an actor walking onto the stage from the wings.

A while later I watched television with neighbours in their house on the occasion of the Coronation of Queen Elizabeth II. The neighbours' television room was packed with other neighbours from the street. Street parties took place on the same day.

With the growth of television in homes, many local cinemas struggled to survive. The cinema in the village next to Aberfan was called the 'bug house' for obvious reasons. Merthyr, four miles away, had four cinemas; I went to all during my teens. The Castle cinema in Merthyr had films on Saturday morning for children and teenagers; they were mainly Westerns.

Our most humorous cinema event was just a few years ago when my wife and I went to see the Abba film *Mamma Mia*. We had premiere reclining seats. On the way out I mentioned to the assistant how comfortable the reclining seats were. The answer was, 'You were sitting on a broken seat, that's why they reclined!'

In my late teens, with two friends, I started going to dance halls. We were all the same age and in the same class in secondary school. Victor – Victor because he was born on Victory Day marking the end of the war on 8th May 1945 - and Merfyn. Victor was tall with black tight curly hair; Merfyn was just a little taller than me, with striking blond hair that remained blond into old age. Merfyn and I were vainer than Victor. Bright colourful ties were my vanity signature piece. I looked much younger than Victor and Merfyn. It is only now, at seventy-eight, that my young face is paying off.

To hide my young appearance, I grew a beard to look older. I shaved it off forty years later to look younger! I now have a designer stubble that comes and goes. My son hates it, and so does my 103-year-old mother. During the second part of the sixties, I had a pencil beard like Mike d'Abo, the trendy Manfred Mann group member. Much later, in an attempt to look serious and politically left-wing, I shaped it in the style of Illtyd Harrington, a Welshman and the Chairman of the Greater London council (1981-1984). One painful consequence of having two friends who were better looking was that I seldom approached an attractive girl for a dance. Playing safe avoided rejection.

We were close friends, all with our girlfriends whom we would later marry. We agreed that we would be best man at each other's wedding. Victor married first, with me as the best man. So the agreement had begun. But I broke the agreement, and my friend from Rolls Royce was my best man, and I was his. The agreement, if followed through, would have had Merfyn being best man to me, and Victor best man to Merfyn. I had left Aberfan behind and living a new life in London but breaking the best man agreement was unforgivable.

All dancing involved holding hands with your partner – always a girl. Girls might dance with each other, but never boy with boy. It was well before the liberation of same-sex association in public or private. Homosexuality had only become legal in 1967. In the valleys homosexuality remained hidden until well into the 1970s.

There were two ways of getting a partner to dance; one was to ask if she would like to dance; the other was to *tap* her male partner on his shoulder. The tap was an instruction for the man to give way and let the *new* man dance with the girl. Sometimes the tapped man would refuse to give way to let him take over the dance with his partner. It might be the cue for a fight. I was always nervous about tapping, just in case the man refused to allow me to take over his partner. If I was tapped, I would immediately give way, much safer that way! As I gave way on one occasion I said, 'I didn't like her anyway', to which he angrily replied, 'Why what's wrong with her? She's my girlfriend'. Better an angry reply than a fight, I thought.

The first dance hall we went to was in Aberfan. Unlike most other dance halls, the Aberfan dance hall was newly built in a modern style and not converted from an old cinema. Old style cinemas were finding it difficult to stay open as people bought televisions. People came from all around to dance in the Aberfan dance hall, which had its resident band.

In Merthyr town the first dance hall was a converted cinema. It was The Palace, the name of the former cinema. I'd had my first car by now, and with this came a new-found status and, my word, did I need status. So, each Friday, the three of us would go to The Palace in my car, an Austin A40. I remember The Palace for two reasons. It was where I met my first wife, and it was the first time I'd seen a glitter ball revolving. It is there that I first saw Tom Jones, or Tommy Woodward, as he was then. Even then, in the early 1960s, he stood out as the best singer The Palace had had.

The music of the late post-war 1950s was beginning to roll over to a new generation in the 1960s. Ballroom dancing began to fade. In came the jive. I jived like no other, and I still can, but I have difficulty finding a girl in her seventies with sufficient lung capacity to complete just one jive! Being an outstanding 'jiver' gave me the status I had craved for, yet again. Girls wanted to jive with me. Gone were the days when I was too shy to invite a girl to dance for fear of rejection. My inhibitions would be no more. I was better than anyone I knew at the jive; well, better than most. My dormant exhibitionism hit the roof, or at least came close to the glitter ball.

The jive replaced traditional ballroom dancing almost overnight though it continued for a while longer in Cardiff City Hall. On one Saturday evening I took a culture leap into the sophistication of Cardiff City Hall. Girls dressed differently from valley girls; they had cocktail dresses. They spoke differently. They would waltz and do the foxtrot. Luckily, I could just about waltz, but the foxtrot was beyond me. I invited a girl to waltz, she answered, 'Yes of course'. 'Yes of course' was a response I had not heard when asking for a jive in Merthyr. I had spoken with a Cardiff girl; this was no small event. My valley accent had passed the test. My confidence was growing, but only just. I needed

30

more practice at honing my sophistication! The Pageant Rooms in Penarth provided the opportunity to practise my increasing sophistication, so I thought, though I was still well short of aplomb! Penarth had a reputation of wealth; lawyers lived there, so did academics and others of the professional class. It was at The Pageant rooms that I knew I had such bad dandruff. The Pageant room dance floor had an ultraviolet crystal ball, a spotlight for spotting dandruff. This was a serious risk to my new sartorial appearance.

Then a brand-new dance venue opened in 1963. It was called a nightclub, not a dance hall. It was located right in the centre of Cardiff, in a converted cinema. It was Top Rank. The new world had arrived. I could not know it then, but it was the beginning of the swinging sixties. The liberation of the post-World War Two baby boomers had arrived. Everything about it sparkled. The music pumped out Motown music for a new generation. It was the sixties, with a new style of clothes, yet I wore a lounge suit, well, at least for a while. The lavatories were called bathrooms. There was a balcony. The décor of the 1950s was swept away. Cardiff City football players went there. I was rubbing shoulders with famous people, and I had my own teeth. Had I been ten years older I might not have had my own teeth. In 1969 the age of majority went from twenty-one to eighteen. It was not unusual when the age of majority was twenty-one for parents to give their adult (child) a full set of false teeth This was because twenty-one was the cut-off age for free dental treatment. Solution, out with the old, in with new. Goodbye dentist!

Needless to say, I've had many friends throughout my life. I had school friends, friends going through adolescence, adulthood friends, colleagues, and friends made in retirement. If I populated a friendship graph of life's friends and friendships, it would show that it has increased from primary school, peaking between the early 20s to mid-30s, plateauing in middle age, then dipping a little into retirement but not too much, with an increase in new friends. My 20s and mid-30s were a most personally rewarding period with friends and family.

The period spanned great social friendships, many shared with my wife. It was a time of exploring my popularity with several overlapping groups. Almost all of it was fuelled by alcohol. Friends were of a complete mix of age and occupations. The mix of alcohol and humour was intoxicating. Had there been a UK prize for one-liners, all my friendship groups would have shared gold, silver, and platinum medals. I did, however, keep on drinking too much into early old age. I am now abstemious. One remark was particularly humorous and would have been awarded the top prize of the period. I asked a good friend about the well-being of her husband in a polite and routine manner. She replied, 'He's not at all well today. He felt so ill he couldn't go to work.' I questioned why, to which she replied, 'He went to a funeral yesterday.' What she failed to say was that his 'illness' was being hung-over from going to the pub with a party of mourners after the funeral.

I made many friends working at Rolls Royce, two in particular. One was from a working-class home in Acton, West London, and the other was an Australian from Brisbane. My London friend and I became each other's best man at our weddings. We would meet in a pub in Islington every Thursday, travelling in one car. Occasionally one of our friends would be serving drinks behind the bar. He was hopeless at giving change and would only charge for one pint of beer, even though several would be ordered! I made several good friends through our Thursday evening meetings.

We had different backgrounds - West London and South Wales, and we were keen to explore the influences on our differences. On our return from the pub, we would spend time, which seemed like hours, talking about our politics. I was outrageously left-wing, and my friend outrageously far-right, unable to come to terms with the Windrush generation, as an example. I was fearlessly opposed to grammar schools and public schools. I was a strong advocate for the rapid increase in comprehensive secondary schools. These differences became too much to hold the friendship together as we grew older.

My Brisbane friend was 'doing' Europe. It was he who wanted me to go to Israel to live in a kibbutz for a while. I turned down his request. Not going to Israel is one of the greatest regrets in my life. He returned after a year and came back to Rolls Royce. For a short time, when recovering from laryngitis, he stayed with my parents in Aberfan when

I returned to London. The rubble of the Aberfan was there at the end of our street.

On one occasion, I arranged for us to go underground at the pit, the spoils of which led to the Aberfan disaster. Experiencing underground was frightening. Going down in the cage to traverse to the coal face with our guide – a collier – allowed us to experience the working conditions of coal miners. For much of the journey underground we had to walk hunched. At the coal face, we could do no more than kneel. Our guide switched off the lamps for us to experience total blackness. My friend and I are still in touch, and we will meet up when I'm in Brisbane visiting my son and his family.

I had another group of friends, mainly teachers from Wales. During the period, and many years before, London attracted newly qualified teachers. I was introduced to the group by a childhood friend who lived four houses away in Aberfan. We would meet at weekends, having no idea where I would end up at the end of the night, but so what; sofas make a comfortable bed when under thirty years of age. If I stayed out on a Sunday night, I would take my clothes for work on Monday. When working as a mechanic my work clothes were overalls. When I became a technician, the clothes would be suit, tie, shirt, underpants, socks, shoes, toothbrush. My suit, made by Austin Reed, became known as my night suit, and when I placed it for the morning, it inevitably produced a humorous comment. It came in handy on another occasion when a fond friend asked me to accompany her to the celebration ball on finishing her teaching qualification.

In London I was at an age when I could cope with burning the candle at both ends. However, there was a particular strain caused by returning to Merthyr too often at weekends to be with my fiancée. We had been courting for nine years before we got married. This should have been a warning of what was to come. It proved to be a shared error of judgement. But it is an example of my fear of letting go; letting go of what I'm not sure, for it rang counter to the freedom I sought so desperately in moving to London.

I enjoyed deep friendships with women, occasionally slipping into a dalliance; and this has been one of the greatest pleasures of life. I had one particularly good friend, who became a Head Teacher at a London primary school. It was a match of humour, and I continue to wonder how life turned out for her. I doubt if I ever will know, however. [Since writing the first edition of this book in 2021, we have made contact with one another and now we email each other frequently.] When I think of friends, emotions come rushing in. They are friends that have been special to me at different times in my life. The emotion of longing is painful with the passing of time.

4: Family

Happiness is having a large, loving, caring, close-knit family in another city

George Burns

My mother was born in Taff Street, Merthyr Vale, where she attended the local school and chapel. When my mother was eight years old her father, an ostler underground, died aged forty from a stroke, leaving her mother, aged thirty-five, with three young children to support. Her grandmother's mother lived in Beaufort where her father was a hot blast fireman. Her mother came from Pembrokeshire. My mother's father was from Llanfyllin, Montgomeryshire.

My distant maternal grandmother worked as a collier underground. The Coal Mines Act was passed in 1842 and stopped all females and children under 18 years of age from underground working. From 1843 the act was extended so that all women had to stop working underground.

A century later my mother, in an entrepreneurial spirit, decided to open a shop in the front room of our house, selling wool. This bold risk was my mother's desperate initiative to supplement my father's sickness benefit, a result of his incapacity to remain in employment due to the severe leg injury that led to his right leg's amputation at the age of forty-two, as I mention below.

In due course the domestic 'shop' was moved to more appropriate retail premises in the centre of Aberfan. These days the clothes my mother sold would be called designer clothes. The shop sold almost everything a woman would want. Clothes ranged from clothes for babies and children, coats, dresses, hats, stockings – affordable tights were not available for several years later - shoes, underwear, raincoats, and adornments. My mother knew her customers well. She knew their sizes, tastes and what they could afford. If a customer wanted clothes for a special occasion, such as a family wedding, my mother would discuss the style of dress with the customer. She would show her a sample rig-out. My mother might buy the whole ensemble for the customer, just as they had discussed.

To help customers with their purchases, she set up a 'club'. The 'club' would be used for customers to pay over an agreed period. My father would call on customers weekly, collecting payments. I would often accompany him. Her customers extended beyond the village and would often be from other valleys and towns. After several successful years, when the adjoining shop became vacant, my parents bought it, and had the two shops knocked into one. They rented out the rooms above the new shop as a home. One room became a hair salon and was let out to a hairdresser. It was this room that my mother allowed the Red Cross to use during the Aberfan disaster. I say more about the Aberfan disaster in Chapter 5.

Friends became agents and sold clothes in factories and offices and other places where they worked. My mother would go to London to buy from small wholesalers and makers of clothes. There were times when I would go with her. Once, we went on the Pullman train service. It was luxurious and faster than other express trains. I would calculate the train's speed by the frequency of the wheel clicks on the rail joints. It kept me occupied throughout the journey, with the trip being tremendously exciting.

Over time my parents bought two houses in the village and rented them. They were able to buy new cars, but they always bought modest cars.

The shop and salon were sold when my mother was seventy, when she retired. Business declined with the new owner, since my mother was no longer there to advise customers. The new owner asked my mother to return to work in the shop. She did so for a couple of years, until she broke her hip rushing to get to the shop after lunch. My mother became known as 'Gwyneth the Shop'. At the age of 103 she is as bright as a button, has a wonderful memory and doesn't miss a trick.

My father's ancestors originated from West Wales. As far back as I can accurately trace the Davies family, their roots lie in Llangynog, Carmarthenshire. My four times grandfather was born there in 1776.

The family were agricultural labourers renting a smallholding. By 1852 the family appears to have moved to Abercanaid, near Merthyr, where my great grandfather William was born that same year. He married Margaret and by the age of thirty they already had six children. Their son John was my grandfather. He married Morfydd, my grandmother, a domestic servant. She was the daughter of John Howells, also a miner from Incline Top, Penydarren. My grandfather's claim to fame was that he played the trombone in Cyfarthfa Brass Band, but like so many of his neighbours and extended family he spent his working life as a collier. He died in 1936 from septicaemia resulting from a wound he had received underground when his crowbar slipped. He was just fifty-five.

My parents met on a 'promenade'. Nowadays this would imply a path by the seaside but at that time it was also the name given to a stroll on a Sunday afternoon taken by young people with the purpose of catching the eye of the opposite sex. They married and set up home in Aberfan Road, where my mother still lives, with my sister and her husband living next door. My father at the time was working in the Kayser Bondor hosiery factory. His problem with his leg meant he did not pass the medical examination to join the armed services, so he continued to work throughout the war in Kayser Bondor. During that period there was a switch from making fashion nylon stockings to stockings for women in the armed services. He became the union representative, yet he said to me more than once that he didn't enjoy reporting back to a large group of his colleagues.

My father was an outstanding amateur footballer who turned professional for Plymouth Argyle. At his final amateur game playing for Aberdare Thursdays – so called because all shops at the time closed on Thursday afternoon - he broke his leg. It was an absolute tragedy for both my mother and father. There my father's promising footballing career ended.

My father's leg was not set correctly by the hospital doctor, and some twenty-years later, thrombosis developed, and he had his leg amputated at the age of forty-two. Whenever we went to the seaside he would step in and out of the sea for hours to cool his legs. He appeared to accept the amputation. However, a few years ago, my mother told me how he suffered psychologically with periods of depression. My suffering was an embarrassment watching him walk with a crutch while waiting for his prosthetic leg. I was on holiday in Bournemouth with my parents and their friends, my father walking a few steps behind, and I turned around to see my father with crutches. I was disturbed and wondered how he felt walking in public on crutches with one leg. His turn for embarrassment came when I pushed him the first time he agreed to go out in a wheelchair; he was seventy-five. When he was eighty he found it increasingly difficult to walk unaided. He was successful in his request for a mobility scooter, but then he failed the NHS scooter driving test. He was deeply saddened with the realisation that finally his independence outside of home was no more.

His long-lost wish was to be an accountant. As it was, he began his working life in a shoe shop in Aberdare, the town where he broke his leg. He would walk four miles over the mountain every day from Abercanaid to Aberdare. His last job was working as a librarian in Aberfan. He spent the rest of his working life doing 'the books' for my mother's shop. He maintained a rational disposition and acted as a check on my mother's propensity to take risks in business, and to be less considered generally. Though of a rational disposition, I never did work out why he disliked the Queen Mother and Bruce Forsyth in equal measure! He did feel proud that he declined an invitation to become a Freemason; this is an example of his rational disposition, as far as I am concerned.

My father would often remark on his pleasure in our relationship and contrasted it with the distant relationship he had with his father. Though he never said it, I know that he wished I was much better at football! I kissed his body on his deathbed, whispering you've been a wonderful father, with all the love a son had for his father. I am proud that he is number eighteen on the register of members of the male voice choir formed in the village after the Aberfan disaster. One of my closest friends joined this choir at the same time. He was in the choir that sang at my father's funeral. My father had a prolonged death, and had it not been for medical intervention he would have died a couple of years earlier. My mother, sister and I lived with the dread of the next ring of the phone. They were at his bedside when he died but I was at work. My career continued to dominate my life, and so it did the moment my father died. I was hesitant about telling my mother and sister that I needed to attend important meetings during the period of mourning. It was not considered respectful to continue with regular life in the days before a funeral in the valleys. I went into college twice, once to chair a critical meeting with trade union representatives, and the other to sit on an appointment panel. I was *present* at each meeting showing no sign of bereavement, though I was in emotional numbness. It was an emotion I had not hitherto experienced as an adult, yet I had instigated the conflicting emotions, and was relieved that I had coped.

My home was safe and comfortable but despite evidence of popular music and popular culture, there were no books. The closest I got to reading the news was the *Daily Mirror, Saturday Football Echo* and the weekend *Reveille*, a lowbrow magazine. Political programmes on television I would watch with my father. It initiated my interest in politics and current affairs. My limited cultural hinterland is still with me, but that's my fault for not exposing myself sufficiently to high culture. There was unadulterated love, though learning to share emotions proved more difficult.

Both my parents were Christians, but neither attended chapel regularly, though my mother did go more than my father. As my father came close to death, at the age of ninety-two, there was no talk about where his ashes would be scattered. I did not have a view regarding this disposal, but my mother and sister agreed on the best location. Three factors influenced their final decision. Firstly, it should be in the village where my father was born. Secondly, because he was a good footballer it should be on a football pitch, and thirdly, because he played his early years at Abercanaid football ground, his ashes should be scattered at the foot of one of the goalposts at the Abercanaid ground.

Recalling these sentiments, I am reminded of another case of funeral ashes. During the time I taught at Merthyr College there was a doorman who was extremely popular, with a dry sense of humour, who sadly died before retiring. His wife asked if his ashes could be scattered on the college grounds. The day of the funeral came, and it was agreed that they would be scattered by the caretaker in the college grounds. Many of us viewed the occasion from the college third floor. As the caretaker scattered the ashes, the wind changed direction, with the ashes blowing on the caretaker's face. The doorman would have chuckled.

When I was growing up it was customary throughout the South Wales valleys to hate Winston Churchill. The story is that he had ordered the troops to break the miners' strike in Tonypandy, though one might have thought the order was given yesterday, so strong was the hostile feeling throughout the region. Churchill's responsibility for ordering the troops to Tonypandy remains a strongly disputed topic but in the valleys of South Wales one can still see a hatred towards Conservatives that can be traced back to the riots of 1910. My own parents remained Labour voters, even though in terms of their relative prosperity through owning two businesses, they were not typical Labour voters for the period. But they would always be proud of being working class, despite the fact that many of their friends were lower middle class, at least if the matrix of occupation is used.

It was only recently that my mother told me that she and my father considered emigrating to Australia under the 'Ten-pound pom' scheme. The scheme was a joint initiative between the UK and Australia to increase the population. Some families made their life in Australia; others came back several years later. My mother claims she wanted to go but my father didn't. My father wanted to emigrate to Canada, where there was a similar scheme in operation to increase the population, but my mother didn't want to go there. The only thing that I can be sure about is my mother's selective memory, which is highly honed.

My father would politely manage my mother's malapropisms, in company at least. One famous malapropism was when she asked for *asbestos* soup when she meant asparagus soup. Having said this, I think I may have inherited my mother's skill of verbal blunders. On one occasion, two of my grandchildren were sitting in the back seats of the car and they asked if I would order a McDonald's McFlurry ice cream at a McDonald's drive-through. They still laugh at me asking for a McFlurry *breakfast* instead of ice-cream! In the early 1970s my train

40

from London was late due to a signal failure near to the Severn tunnel. This gave me an extra hour drinking time in the buffet. As I approached Top Rank, in Cardiff, where my friends were patiently waiting, I spluttered, 'Sorry I'm late, there was a *fignal sailor.*'

I was named Brenig without my parents' deference to its etymology. My parents decided on the name when returning from the New Theatre, Cardiff, where the first name of one actor was Brenig. My mother was heavily pregnant with me at the time. There is a Llyn Brenig reservoir in North Wales. There is a Brenig tributary of the River Teifi, which runs through the market town of Tregaron in West Wales. Unbeknown to my mother, the etymology of Brenig is that it is formed from Bran, which means 'crow' or 'raven' in Welsh (I prefer the notion of being named after a raven than a common crow, I have to say) but is also a personal name and *ig* a diminutive suffix. Also, Brenig is a district of Bornheim, Germany and is a German surname. In fact, on a study tour of Germany, I came across a motor vehicle service centre with a sign BRENIG. Welsh or German, it's too late to change it now. I'm seventy-eight. Though, perhaps I should change it; without a capital B, *brenig* is a term for a geeky kid in the Urban Dictionary. However, a good friend, a biologist, when researching for his S4C (Welsh language television channel) programme was reminded that 'brenig' is the Welsh language translation of 'limpet'. Known characteristics of limpets are resilience and tenacity. I'm happy to be associated with resilience and tenacity.

My London friends were not necessarily interested in etymology, but Brenig was a name they had not previously heard – two unfamiliar linked syllables seemed just too much for them, though there are plenty of disyllabic English names of course. Whatever, Brenig became Bryn and the problem was solved.

***

Having children and grandchildren are happy events in life. The birth of a child may be the emotional high point in confirming manhood and women's fertility. We were liberal parents, especially for the time, in the valleys of South Wales. Dr Spock's book on parenting strongly influenced our parenting; the book attracted great interest amongst (middle-class I assume) parents, with the theory of putting the child at the centre of shared actions and decisions from an early age. The idea advanced by Dr Spock was radically different from traditional notions of a strict upbringing of children by many parents, certainly in the South Wales valleys.

When our children were toddlers, they were not chastised with a smack; if they did something they ought not to have done, we would explain firmly why the action was inappropriate. All our friends would remark, with bewilderment, that we would not smack our children. These days there is legislation in Wales that prohibits the smacking of children.

My wife was a wonderful mother. She ensured our children took school seriously and looked after-them for long daytime periods while I was studying. With the birth of our son, she gave up her dental technician job and remained home until they finished schooling.

Both our children gained university degrees: our son, a BA in Product Design, then an MBA, our daughter, a BA in Humanities. The two knew how much I wanted them to get degrees. Our son did his first degree on leaving school and his MBA on returning to Wales from Australia for a short while. After completing his MBA, he returned to Australia. It was while doing his MBA that his dyslexia was diagnosed; he was forty years of age. My wife and I acted as tutors to help them with study skills, analysis and essay writing. I grew much closer to my son when it dawned on him that I knew something about apostrophes!

During his time returning from Australia, my son opened a shop selling reconditioned bikes. My daughter started higher education twice and finally gained her degree through the Open University at early middle age whilst bringing up three young children. Later she opened several businesses in hospitality. It seemed that they both had acquired the entrepreneurial skills of my mother.

We have eight grandchildren between us. All except the youngest are in their teenage years. The five who live in South Wales, three in Merthyr and two in Barry, attend Welsh-medium schools; two are in Brisbane, with the youngest in East London. Our Brisbane grandchildren went to Welsh-medium nursery school, before returning to Australia. Grandchildren bring so much pleasure and laughter. On one occasion, on my birthday, I had a box of kisses. They'd asked me a few days before what I wanted for my Birthday, and I replied 'a box of kisses'. They presented me with a closed box. I opened it, and there was a box full of kisses. They had spent hours cutting up a hundred or so square white paper with the imprint of lipstick lips.

My father-in-law was wonderfully humorous; he was a British Rail *poacher* and would do anything to save money. My son loved him, as did my daughter. My son, in particular, is grateful for the lifelong practical skills he learned from his grandfather, who worked as an engine driver for British Rail. This could be deduced from the items in his home, from cutlery to toilet paper, which all bore the stamp 'British Rail'. He had garden gnomes scattered in the front and back gardens. On one occasion, he dropped one gnome, causing the legs to smash into smithereens. Not to waste the upper body, he placed it back in the same place, but this time with only the upper body. Towards the end of his time as a train driver on the valley lines, new signal boxes were introduced. The wooden steps of the old signal boxes were taken to the goods yard of Merthyr station. Not to waste one of the sets of wooden steps, which was designed with an elevation of 40 degrees, he had it delivered to the rear garden, which had an elevation of 50 degrees. The result was that when you walked up the steep rear garden it had the impression underfoot of walking downwards!

5: The Aberfan Disaster

Where was God that fateful day

In a place called Aberfan

Ron Cook

I was twenty-two at the time of the Aberfan disaster in October 1966, I had attended both the primary and secondary school where the pit spoil smothered one hundred and sixteen children and twenty-eight adults. News travelled quickly globally. Having one of the few telephones in the village, my mother called the colliery immediately to tell the person who answered the phone what she had been told by those rushing from the school. The person on the other end of the call dismissed my mother's message. Despite her advanced years my mother clearly remembers the phone call incident. Subsequently my mother was interviewed by one of the inquiry investigators to ascertain the veracity of her remarks. She was not able to be precise about the time of her call to the pit and she learned no more about what had happened. She attended to several of the children who were brought out alive, taking them into her house to be washed before they were taken home.

There were seven tips a short walk above the schools on the mountainside. While in primary and secondary school, teachers would occasionally remark that those tips would come down one day. The weather on the day of the disaster did not prefigure tragedy, however. It was a typical autumn morning: a low mist lying over the village with bright blue sky above the mist. I had left the village at 8.20 am to drive to my apprenticeship day-release class in Pontypridd College (a college where 19 years later I would be vice-principal). At approximately 11.00 am my teacher said to me, 'Davies, you're from Aberfan. You should go home.' I was given no reason why I should go but as I drove the fifteen miles to my home, I saw ambulances coming in the opposite direction. I turned to leave the A470 to take the road into Aberfan when a policeman stopped me and would not let me take the usual way home.

There are only two ways of entering Aberfan, one from the north and one from the south. My regular entry was from the south when approaching it from Pontypridd. I can't fully remember my emotions when a policeman stopped me from entering the village where I had lived all my life. I became increasingly anxious and quickly drove three miles north to enter the village that way. As I approached Aberfan, a policeman directed me to pull over and park about two hundred yards away from my home. I knew something terrible had happened. I got to my house, still not knowing what had happened, where my mother told me of the unfolding disaster.

The tip had come down on the primary and secondary schools. I had been a pupil at both schools from the age of three to fifteen. The magnitude of the disaster unfolded into the evening. Press reporters and radio and television reporters were there in droves. I remember vividly watching Cliff Michelmore, a well-known senior television presenter, standing on the slurry of the tip, making a live news report in the evening of the disaster. As a family we were instructed to leave our home and not to re-enter for four days. I felt like an evacuee as we slept in my grandmother's house. It was a terraced house built for the colliers of Merthyr Vale pit located on a hill directly opposite our home, with the river Taff running between Aberfan and Merthyr Vale. We slept there for three nights until the army allowed us back into our house. The word *evacuee* remains seared in my brain. Getting out of bed and looking across to the disaster scene was an incomprehensible reality, not a bad dream. There was my home in a scene of devastation. Houses and streets were missing. A few flattened tips on the mountain remained.

Charities moved in to help quickly. One charity was the Salvation Army. On returning to my home, on my own, I took the offer of a sandwich and water from them. This act is one of the most lasting memories of my life during the disaster. I was moments from my home. I was well known in the village, but they, the Salvation Army, did not know me. I'm still struggling to express my emotion at taking a sandwich and water from a charity. My house could be seen from the Salvation Army tables, with a soldier standing outside. I can't remember why the soldier, who did not know me, let me enter my home, but he did.

The bodies of the victims were placed in a chapel directly opposite my mother's shop, where she had allowed the Red Cross to provide food for those helping in Bethania chapel. [There is a telling note on Bethania and the decline of chapel goers: several years later a modem chapel was built on the site of Bethania. As I write, in 2023, the chapel has been remained closed for a long while and is now up for sale.] I can see, to this day, a man, whose wife had been a teacher in the primary school, standing outside the chapel doors. It was dusk, he was tall, slim, and handsome standing there as if he was in some poignant scene in a Hollywood movie.

The Duke of Edinburgh visited the day after the disaster. The BBC film clip shows him entering the side entrance of my parents' house on his way to the school. The Queen came a week later on the 29th.

It is reported (in *Town and Country*) that this is the only time she has been seen crying a little in public. According to Sally Bechdel Smith's biography, *Elizabeth the Queen*, the monarch's caution (visiting a week later) wasn't a decision made out of coldness, but rather practicality. "People will be looking after me', she said, according to Smith. "Perhaps they'll miss some poor child that might have been found under the wreckage."

Even today, when together with my mother and sister the disaster is seldom mentioned. I'm not sure of my emotions, other than that my soul won't settle. If the disaster appears in the media, I immediately turn away or turn the TV off. I get disturbed when photographs appear of the disaster in newspapers. I'm not sure if my emotions are genuine, because my loss was not the absolute loss of the bereaved. I have found solace in writing poems at stages in my life. Two written in my old age are presented in the epilogue of this memoir.

The Welsh language television service S4C commissioned a requiem to commemorate fifty years of the disaster. Cantata composed for the anniversary, was played first at a concert in the Millennium Centre, Cardiff. I was disturbed that there was a concert to mark the occasion. I would not go. I saw the concert as entertainment. My emotions were heightened by listening to the composition a little later, and much later

I stiffened myself to view a recording on television. Perhaps it was the use of creative licence that the Cantata included a piece reflecting the silence of birds when uncovering a body and of 'Myfanwy' being sung by the soldiers. Unless the soldiers were Welsh, they would not be familiar with Myfanwy. I was there; it was a myth. The urban legends were repeated by BBC Wales online in advertising the concert. I wrote to BBC Wales, expressing my deep concern, asking them for unequivocal evidence of the advertising material that mentioned 'Myfanwy' and the silence of the birds. It took BBC Wales months to reply, and when they did, they asked if I would wish the material to be removed from their online site. I replied that the decision to remove it was theirs.

The myths also appeared in the Guardian (1.10.16) in an article written by the composer of Cantata, Karl Jenkins:

'The Welsh song "Myfanwy" (written by Joseph Parry from nearby Merthyr Tydfil) was sung by the soldiers who dug for victims…memories and celebrating childhood…. It is said that no birdsong was heard in the hours before or after the tragedy, and so the words "light" and a "bird" provide the textual thread towards the conclusion of the piece…'

Several years after the Aberfan disaster, I was attracted to a hardback novel whose title related to the Free Wales Army, which was not an army as such, but a 'soft' terrorist group of Welsh-speakers, who objected to people from England buying up houses in Welsh language heartlands. An action of the group was to burn down houses bought by the English. On reading the novel, it was clear that the two main themes were the Free Wales Army and the Aberfan disaster, though it was not named as such. A while later I was attracted to a paperback novel with a different yet similar title to the hardback. The paperback book was a new edition of the hardback book. I was annoyed that the author, and publisher, had used the disaster to blatantly promote the book. I wrote to the Editor of *The Western Mail* to explain the promotion of the books and the letter was published.

There are other haunting details I recall. I used to repair cars with a friend in a gully that I had driven down on my way to college the

47

morning of the disaster. A child of my parents' friends would frequently join us watching while we fixed cars there. This child was a victim of the disaster. He was cremated with a few other children. Much later, a permanent monument of ornate arches was built on the mountain, with each arch over a grave for each child. Even closer to home, our neighbour's child was killed. He would frequently come to my home and sit with me in the garden. I also lost a cousin who lived on the same road, Aberfan Road. The Aberfan disaster happened in the final year of my apprenticeship. The child of one of the garage's customers was killed in the disaster. The child's mother never forgave herself for letting the child, who was late for school, walk through the school gates. She is still living with her thought that slurry had already started to engulf the school as she waved goodbye.

Two decades after the Aberfan disaster, following a most acrimonious coal miners' strike, which led eventually to the almost total closure of the coal mining industry across Britain, communities changed instantly. The camaraderie associated with the dangerous work underground was no more. Well paid and skilled work disappeared. In the villages of the South Wales valleys, where the pit was the major employer, there was now high unemployment and desperation in family life. Support groups were formed, and food banks were set up. Wives became the breadwinners in some cases. Much later, many wives gained new-found confidence and went on to study in FE colleges and enter careers previously not known to them. Some became community leaders, having become assertive, without recognising it in themselves. Out of adversity, many of the women were liberated.

I remember well a colleague from the Welsh Development Agency making an insightful remark about the high unemployment rate in the valley coalfields: 'It's pitiful that the unemployed in the South Wales valleys are *chronic employees.*' My colleague was not from the area, yet it often takes an outsider to see what locals cannot see. The valleys, and much of Wales, especially when compared with London and the South East, have a socio-economic culture that does not foster entrepreneurial employment. With much Welsh Government support, Wales has a high failure rate of new independent start-up small companies.

The Government Welsh Development Agency attracted new forms of employment to the valleys, but so many were not well paid and lacked an environment to sustain the former social culture of valley life. Today there is no sign that a pit existed in a village, except for the remaining colliery tips in several villages. There is poor health, including mental health. The valleys of South Wales are more impoverished than a few eastern countries of the European Union. There is little significant inward migration apart from young men, mainly, from countries of the former Europe eastern bloc.

One consequence of a significant lack of inward migration is heard in the language of those children brought up in the valleys. Of course, there are exceptions, but the accent of the young and others who have lived their lives in the valleys can be considered to be so non-standard that their linguistic limitations might inhibit job opportunities, for example, working in the retail sector in Cardiff.

6: Starting Work

*There is no passion in playing small – in settling for a life that is less than you
are capable of living*

Nelson Mandela

Becoming an apprentice motor mechanic in a new garage selling
petrol in Aberfan immediately took away the evident
pointlessness of schooling. Secondary school had been
unfulfilling, with no noteworthy achievement of which I could be
proud. It had not been a happy period in my life. So, an apprenticeship,
and an indentured one at that, gave me kudos with my friends. There
was status having an apprenticeship since they were sought after by
teenage boys; there were fewer apprenticeship trades for young girls.
In hairdressing, for instance, the apprentice would have to pay the hair
salon owner to be trained. To show the scarcity of apprentice
placements in the 1960s, apprenticeships were available to about fifteen
percent of that cohort of young school leavers. For me, I thought, the
apprenticeship offered a secure future that would have influence over
the rest of my life. I had a highly skilled job with career prospects. Why
shouldn't I feel confident and good about myself?

I was the only employee at the garage where I would serve my
apprenticeship. It was owned by two middle-aged brothers-in-law, who
gave the initial letter of their surname to the garage name: J&J Motors.
Both had given up full-time employment to open the garage. Looking
back, it was quite a risk for them. One partner had been a mechanic,
and the other a technician in an aircraft industry factory. They worked
well together. The aircraft industry partner did car servicing and he
learned nothing about car repair for all the period of my apprenticeship.
The mechanic partner and I did the repairs and maintenance. It allowed
me to become a fully competent, skilled motor mechanic, which gave
me much confidence for the next phase of my life.

Shortly after the garage partner left the aircraft industry factory it
closed, and this loss of opportunity for highly skilled men in Merthyr
preceded a significant decline in employment for such workers in the

area. Highly skilled jobs began to be replaced by work for factory operators. The reduction in highly skilled employees has continued to this day. The closure of the famous Hoover factory reduced the number of skilled jobs years later. The period foresaw the rapid decline of skilled occupations in the valleys of South Wales and, taken together with earlier colliery closures, there have been significant changes in the socioeconomic profile of South Wales. To this day, however, memories live on of the relative affluence of valley communities amongst the old.

Changing employment conditions were accompanied by an acceleration of the aspiration of parents for their children. Naturally they wanted a better life for them than working in the pit. One consequence of this led to waves of young newly trained teachers leaving the valleys to cities of England, and particularly to London, as had been the case decades ago.

It was the time of 'baby boomers' starting school, 'baby boomers' being the term used to describe a generation where there was a significant increase in births following men returning home from World War Two. Teacher training colleges expanded rapidly, and new ones were created, to meet the need of filling teaching posts created by the expansion of children needing education. Research carried out by University College Cardiff in the 1960s into the educational achievement level of newly trained teachers and apprentices concluded that apprentices and trainee teachers were of similar cognitive abilities. There is a relationship with this research in the 1960s apropos relative educational achievement of apprentices and trainee teachers. Both forms of employment have become degree occupations.

I worked diligently at the garage, which had quickly become a busy petrol station, the only one in the village. When working on a car, if a vehicle came onto the forecourt, one of us would drop everything to serve petrol. Meeting and communicating with adults frequently helped immensely with my maturity into adulthood; it gave me much confidence, meeting and speaking with people of all ages and status.

On one occasion I used my new-found confidence, to help a customer a little too conscientiously. He ordered a gallon of petrol; I filled the tank full to the brim, but it was a few drops short of the gallon (it was gallons in those days not litres). In my determination to help the customer have the gallon he paid for, I suggested that he start the engine to use what little petrol was needed to have the full gallon. It soon dawned on me how ridiculous my advice was, but it was not soon enough for the customer to burst out laughing. Better it was laughter though, I thought, than me being the butt of his displeasure.

The garage was five minutes from home and was reached by a back street or by the main road, which involved passing the main bus stop in Aberfan. I would take the main road route and leave home in time to pass the bus stop for Merthyr when the queue was sufficiently long for the commuters to see me. I would be in my uniform of brown overalls and proudly walk, knowing the same people in the queue would be there Monday to Friday. My pride in walking past the bus queue reflected my status as an indentured apprentice.

I was known in the village and considered to be mature and a safe pair of hands. There were times when I would be the only one in the garage. Repairing cars, changing tyres, and serving petrol; this was my work, and I was proud of it. These days they would call it multi-skilling. I could count and give the correct change to customers. I learned more arithmetic in two months than twelve years of schooling. I communicated well, and I was not in awe of customers, though my embarrassment at asking the customer to switch on his engine to ensure he had the full gallon of petrol lived on.

One interesting point I observed is the different status attributed to wearing overalls and smart leisure clothes. I noticed many times, whether someone knew me or not, their reaction to me depending on whether I was wearing overalls or leisure wear. Smart leisure wear would be more likely to evoke a more respectable encounter than dirty work overalls.

There was one drawback, the weather. Handling steel tools on cold winter days is torturous. The workshop doors of the garage were almost always open. There was room for a single car, and half a car behind, which meant the garage door could not be closed. Due to health and safety regulations, we were not to work when the temperature was too cold but we did. Rain was a blessing compared to the freezing temperature. Thank goodness there are more days of rain than cold days in the valleys. It rains a lot more in the valleys than the coastal belt thirty miles south. The valleys are beautiful but also claustrophobic, especially when the clouds are low and misty. There were times when I felt hemmed in by the valley. I knew I would not spend all my life in Aberfan, but I had no idea about my career journey.

The hydraulic lift was never serviced. Over time, while working underneath the car, it would slowly slip down. The problem was overcome by leaving the high-pressure air continuously pumping up the hydraulic metal pole. This was a perilous measure, but never considered dangerous enough to have the lift serviced.

One customer named David would always ask for half the car's petrol tank to be filled with high octane (expensive) petrol and the other half with cheaper low octane petrol. He became known as Dai Arf and Arf.

Because I had an indentured apprenticeship, my employer would be in receipt of my progress from my college day-release course. Notice of my examination results was addressed to my bosses. It was August, and I knew my examination results were due. They arrived, and my employers told me that I had failed. I was saddened and surprised. What would my future hold? It was at the end of the day that I was told that they were joking and that I had passed. I have never fathomed out why people play such games. This episode was deeply disturbing.

I was seventeen attending Pontypridd College when I asked the college receptionist if I could take her home in my car. She accepted and I took her home to a village in the Rhondda. We agreed to meet again and set a day for the following week. On returning from work one day that week, my father handed me an opened envelope and I saw that the letter was addressed to me. It was from the college receptionist politely informing me that she had changed her mind about our arranged meeting. I felt highly indignant that my father had opened a personal letter addressed to me; I was seventeen!

In one lesson, while at college, there was an occasion when the teacher thought I was not paying attention because I was talking too much. He turned to me and said: 'Davies, you are wasting your time on this course'. It was twenty years later that I became his boss as the college vice principal. I'm sure he forgot the remark! I was not always inattentive, however, and I went on to pass my apprenticeship examinations. Had I failed, I can't bear to think of what would have happened to me. In addition to the theory examination, I had to be tested on my practical knowledge and skills. The test was conducted in Cardiff Institute of Higher Education, where decades later my wife taught. By this time, it had become a university.

Soon after completing my apprenticeship, I worked in the Merthyr bus garage. It was just four miles from my home in Aberfan, but I was nervous about leaving the garage where the owners had been so kind as to employ me as an indentured apprentice. I was now a certificated skilled mechanic. I had started my apprenticeship as an adolescent and was leaving as a man. I was anxious about telling the owners of the garage that I was leaving. It never dawned on them that I would leave Aberfan. My experience of family enmeshment had extended to my first job. Deciding to leave the Aberfan garage for Merthyr bus garage was the most significant decision of my life thus far. I was twenty-one years of age. I still look back to that decision knowing of my determined desperation to leave Aberfan; a determination that I've honed in all aspects of my life.

It was my first experience of working in a team with a line-manager. I was utterly lost in the expansive working environment of the bus garage. I knew after the first week that the bus garage was not for me. There were many kind, and mature, skilled men who helped me learn and cope with maintaining buses, but there were also a couple of men working there who thrived on bullying and I was one of their victims. They worked as a bullying team of two, reinforcing each other's sniggering at their targets. There was little opportunity to assert one's independence, for attempting to do so would only have given them fertile ground for further insidious remarks and faux laughs.

Even in the mid-60s, the working practices drain on ratepayers' money (community charge) was outrageous. Jobs were timed by the half-day or days. Under no circumstances should a newcomer, like me, complete a job in less than the time allocated to the job. When I served

54

my apprenticeship, once I'd completed a job, I would begin another. In the bus garage, the supervisor would assign a job to skilled staff with respective skills. For instance, a qualified electrician would only do electrical work; repairs to fuel systems were for those skilled in diesel engines; a labourer would service buses but not repair them. All jobs had defined times and it would be heresy to complete a job in less than the specified time. The trade union convenor would admonish newcomers, and I was one of them, if the allotted time for a job was completed in a shorter period. One mechanic who had been there a long time was nicknamed 'the vicar' because he only had enough work for one day a week. The authority bestowed on him by colleagues reveals a deference given to a coterie of *job time enforcers*.

One was not allowed to cross skill areas, even though a skilled mechanic would, for instance, have the skills to replace diesel components, it would be only the designated diesel fitter who could work on diesel components. There were many industrial disputes initiated by powerful trade unions during the decades following World War Two in the UK. If management directed an experienced motor mechanic to repair an electrical fault that was a skilled electrician's responsibility, there would be a demarcation dispute. It would lead to the trade union representative meeting with management to resolve the issue, and many times it led to a strike until the matter was resolved. For decades up to the 1950s the British car industry was the second largest car manufacturer in the world, next to the USA, but demarcation disputes, old production methods and poor management led to the demise of Britain as a mass-production car manufacturer within ten years. Today it lags a lowly fourteenth.

The promotion of an employee in the bus garage was related to his length of service. It had no relationship to competence or management skills. It even extended to bus drivers. The longest serving bus drivers had the privilege of driving on the Cardiff route. The practice of promotion by length of service crippled much of the British print industry in the 1980s. It was Rupert Murdoch, an Australian businessman, who eventually dismantled the practice of promotion by length of service, helped with the emerging new technologies, especially in the field of computing, in early 1986.

Even though I was only employed at the bus garage for a short while, I was elected to be the trade union representative for skilled mechanics. I remained active in the trade union movement throughout my career in the motor industry and in the post-16 education sectors. For instance, I was elected as chair of the Association for College Management (Wales) while employed as a vice-principal. Colleagues, while I was vice principal, asked if I would become the union representative for college managers. I did not accept the role because it would inevitably have meant that I would be in dispute with the college principal, my line-manager. I was nevertheless immensely proud of the confidence colleagues had in me.

In the bus garage, workers would clock on-and-off at the beginning and end of day by punching a card into a box below an integrated clock. It was not unknown for a friend to clock-in a colleague running late. The disrespect workers had for management, and the disrespect management had for workers, was rife in so many public sector organisations. Instances of a breakdown in industrial relationships were commonplace stories in newspapers and the media.

But working life was not all about conflict; there was humour and conviviality too. A siren would indicate when work was to begin in the morning and after lunch and it was the supervisor's duty to press the siren button. He lived about ten minutes from the bus garage, and he would go home for lunch. Occasionally a worker would press the siren button as the supervisor was in sight of the garage. It was a harmless prank, albeit perhaps one designed to underline the lack of respect that the workforce had for organisational discipline. Another anecdote reveals the same thing but shows the workers' humour too. A colleague who lived in a pub got into the habit of coming to work for just four days each week. The garage supervisor admonished him and asked why he frequently came to work four days so many times; he replied, 'Because I can't afford to live on three days.' The most humorous remark I heard when working there was between two colleagues who worked as a team and exchanged banter worthy of a TV comedy programme. One, who had an enormous nose, remarked to his colleague, 'I don't know what's wrong with me today. I'm so tired I could sleep on my nose'. To which the other replied, 'Move over then,

56

there's plenty of room for me'.

Cover for bus breakdowns was through a rota system of two colleagues working during the evening and getting paid the normal hourly rate plus half for every extra hour worked on breakdown cover until all the buses had returned to the depot The payment system was called 'time and a half'. Those on breakdown cover were expected to continue with their daily work into the evening but seldom did this happen. It was not unusual for skilled men to work on their own car during the paid over-time cover. Knowing this ruse, one of the two strategic managers would appear without notice to check on those on overtime working to ensure they were continuing with their day jobs.

These two managers were from Yorkshire. It was not uncommon in the public sector through to the 1980s for town councillors to appoint senior managers from England; this appointment policy was also evident in FE colleges. It was as though applicants and subsequent appointments from England were better suited to the demands of senior strategic management positions than those from Wales. It was an example of lamentable lack of confidence in those already in respective public sectors in Wales. It served to exacerbate harmonious working relationships between management and shop floor workers. There were cases where councillors were terrified that managers, who lived locally, would 'go native' when fulfilling their role as leaders, and would therefore demur from taking difficult decisions. I experienced the threat of 'going native' while a vice principal in the merged college of Pontypridd. There were three senior managers, a principal and two vice principals. My two senior management colleagues, making up the senior management team, had been in their posts for a period much shorter than me. They were nervous, and warned me tangentially, not to go 'native'. It took a short while for me to understand what was meant by 'going native'. For me 'going native' was my way of managing, with no threat to the senior management of the college.]

On one occasion, when I was with a colleague on the breakdown cover rota at the bus garage, I went out to get fish and chips. We were sitting on a rest bench when one of the senior managers walked into the garage workshop and, in a strong Yorkshire accent, loudly admonished us for eating our fish and chips in cover time. 'Dear chips at time and a half', he proclaimed, but not a word of discipline followed; such was the impotence of senior management in the public sector, set against the strength of trade unions.

There was a most despicable action taken by the diesel fuel specialist. In his greed for overtime, he planned that a bus chartered by Merthyr Labour Club would develop problems on the return journey in the evening when he was on call-out, so that he would be paid at time-and-a-half for the repair job. As planned, the bus broke down full of exhausted parents and children after a day in Barry Island.

Working in the bus garage gave me the chance to drive buses. Just as boys wished to be train drivers in the age of steam engines, I wished to drive buses. Double decker buses had an open area at the rear for entry and alighting. It was not uncommon for passengers running to get on the bus to jump on while the bus was leaving the bus stop, although in doing so some people were injured and even killed. Buses had conductors, who issued tickets to ensure all passengers paid their fare.

When taking a bus out on a test run, a colleague needed to sit downstairs in the passenger area to prevent a person from getting on thinking it was a bus in service. On one occasion, when I was out on a test, in order to let an oncoming lorry pass I had to stop. Coincidentally I was at a bus stop. A passenger stepped onto the bus. It was when we entered the bus station that the man rang the bell to get off. When we took the bus into the garage my colleague said to me, 'You know him, do you?' I replied, 'No, I thought you knew him.' The event lightened an otherwise lazy day.

On another occasion, towards the end of my period in the bus garage I was returning to work after my lunch break in my MG midget. I had been to the centre of town when I saw a friend. I stopped and asked if I could give her a lift. She said she was going to the tax office, so she got into my car. I drove off to the bus garage and on approaching the bus garage she nervously asked, 'Where are you taking me?' I replied, 'To the tax office as you said on getting into the car'. She responded, 'Not this tax office'. I had taken her to the vehicle tax office which was located near to the entry of the bus garage, a distance from the town centre. She retorted, 'Thank you for the lift, but I meant the HM tax office where I work'; this was in the town centre. We chuckled as I turned around and took her back to her office; I could, though, sense the relief on her face. We stayed friends!

Most staff would take lunch in the mess room, sitting in positions they had sat in for years. Occasionally some would start aiming their used lunch paper at those who would reciprocate the game. I was bemused by this behaviour and there were times when I would join others not having lunch in the mess. I was not used to working in a factory culture and couldn't get out quickly enough. Time was unproductive in the bus garage. It provided an opportunity for games, usually at the expense of colleagues, such as the trick played on the mayor's chauffeur. He was well dressed, tall and slim, with an expensive double-breasted navy suit and shiny black shoes. On one occasion he stood against the side of a double-decker bus. The bus was over a walk-in service pit. There he stood with the heels of his shoes exposed to the mechanic servicing the bus; I was there too. My co-mechanic painted his heels with white gloss paint. Off the chauffeur went, walking smartly through the workshop for all to see his shiny black and white shoes.

The deregulation of bus services in 1986 led to the closure of the bus garage. The site is now a small housing estate. Only a historian of bus travel will know of the working practices hidden in the garage.

However, incidents such as the ones I mention confirmed in my mind that I should leave the bus garage. At that stage in my life, I knew my reasons to leave were more complex than was caused by paper throwing in the garage mess. Although my main motivation was *flight*, I had the determination to *fight* for my independence.

It was during this period that I bought my first *Guardian* newspaper to assuage my emotions. I bought it in John Menzies book stall at Merthyr railway station. I felt a fully-fledged lefty and was beginning to feel confident with my views on life. I was now reading a *quality* newspaper. It was in another newspaper, however, a now defunct tabloid *The Daily Sketch*, that I saw an advertisement for a job as a motor mechanic for Rolls Royce in London.

I got an interview; my first, because I had not been interviewed for employment in the bus garage; such was the sloppiness of employment practices. The Rolls Royce personnel officer sent me a letter a couple of days later, with the offer of employment, and a request that I start as soon as possible. Because I was on a weekly wage in the bus garage, not a monthly salary, I was able to start within a few weeks. My fiancée appeared not to object to my moving to London, though it is testament to my insensitivity that I never thought too much about her feelings. My parents were not happy; enmeshment exercising its powers yet again, even at my age of twenty-two.

7: Rolls Royce

At 60 mph the loudest noise in the Rolls Royce engine comes from the electric clock

David Ogilvy

I started working at Rolls Royce, Motor Car Division, in London, on 30th September 1967, a fortnight after my twenty-second birthday. I drove to work in my MG Midget convertible sports car. It was the day BBC Radio 1 began broadcasting. The presenter Tony Blackburn played 'Flowers in the Rain' by The Move. I was driving into a new world and the music chimed with my excitement and freedom. I was an independent man at last, already in tune with the culture of the 'swinging sixties' and I knew it. I had joined the post war adult generation – a baby boomer.

On the first day at Rolls Royce an experienced mechanic was assigned to manage my induction and to be my coach for a while. It was so different from beginning my employment in Merthyr bus garage, where I just walked into the workshop, eventually found my locker and simply started work. I soon realised that fellow motor mechanics were eager to uphold the reputation of Rolls Royce. Within a few weeks, I knew everyone within my assigned section and a few colleagues in other parts of the factory. A colleague from Wales, much older than me, had a wonderful Welsh accent modulated by living for forty years in London. I'm not one to reflect on Wales through rose coloured spectacles and neither was he, but it was simply pleasant to share a social culture through our respective generations.

It was delightful working in Rolls Royce with so much banter and fun. The working culture was very different from the Merthyr bus garage. There were many layers of management, too many, but this was not unusual for the time. Our middle-aged line manager dressed well, in keeping with his position. He was bald. One Monday morning he entered the workshop wearing a wig, only to be greeted by a cry from a colleague, in his West London voice, 'Morning baldy'.

The maintenance factory, which was located on Scrubs Lane with Wormwood Scrubs prison in sight, had three floors and an adjacent new building. In this new building, where I started my time, about fifteen skilled motor mechanics worked, mostly from west London but a couple from Ireland and one from Australia. My Australian colleague became a close friend and still is to this day. I made another good friend, and we became each other's best man at our weddings.

I was struck by the attention to quality and safety. There was a safety operator whose job was to check that wheels were safely replaced with the correct torque. There was a tester, whose job it was to take the car for a short test run before it was made ready for return to the owner. The workshop had a dedicated cleaner, George, whose job was mainly to remove oil from the workshop floor. George was visually impaired, with glasses with thick prisms. On one occasion he slipped on the oil he was employed to remove. Spontaneous laughter from colleagues was barely muffled by concern for George's wellbeing.

It was such a stimulating time working on the shop floor as a motor mechanic. There was a special tool for every complex operation. The creeper boards had leather headrests; a luxurious headrest better than some South Wales sofas, or settees as they are called by many in the valleys of South Wales. On completion of a job, there was another one immediately. No wasting of time, as in the Merthyr bus garage.

The job card for each job would indicate the work to be undertaken and provide the car's owner details.

Two years later, I was promoted to the post of technician, which was an office-based role. I'd progressed from dirty overalls to a clean white coat. I had longed to have a job outside of dirty overalls. It was there that I first caught sight of a Boeing 747, or jumbo jet as it became known, in January 1970. I progressed from the workshop floor to an office that gave me a self-appointed high status, including lavatories with standard cubicle doors. Doors of lavatories in the workshop floor for mechanics were of the stable door kind. There were separate areas in the canteen, though the range of food for office staff was the same. I felt proud. Amongst my jobs was to keep a technical library up to date; it was no more than a large filing cabinet but keeping a library at

Rolls Royce remained on my CV for a while!

A more exciting job was a one-off. The gearbox in the Silver Shadow model was overheating; I examined the problem. It was not for me to permanently remedy the problem, but it was for me to try a few options that might lead to a permanent solution. I took the option of taking the gearbox oil through a radiator under the wing and back into the gearbox. I tested it along Regent Street in the West End. I did this because the ambient temperature is higher in the city. It worked; the gearbox oil temperature was lower. It was a make-do-and-mend option, not a fully permanent remedy. Heath Robinson would have been pleased with me. While driving down Regent Street a car from behind mounted the pavement; the driver was unconscious. I dread to think of the consequences had the car driven into the Rolls Royce.

In the early summer of 1969, while still a mechanic on the workshop floor, I received a job card with the 'owner' HRH. My job was to service one of the Queen's official cars in preparation for Prince Charles's investiture in Caernarfon Castle, North Wales on 1st July 1969. This moment of luck was too good to miss.

As I lay there underneath the HRH car, I struggled to resist writing in white chalk on the chassis 'Free Wales'. My resistance didn't last long. I then wrote 'Rhyddau Cymru' in green chalk, green being the colour used by Cymdeithas, the Welsh Language Society, though I felt safer using chalk rather than the paint they used to inscribe their slogans. The BBC video clip of the Queen's car entering the castle is currently on YouTube and I recently played it at one of our Friday evening story-telling sessions. The story-telling evenings began on Zoom, due to COVID-19, and continued on Zoom. A couple from West Virginia, who are part of the story telling group, were most interested in my story. My Australian friend continues to dine out on the tale, suitably embellished.

One of the royal cars would go ahead of the Queen when visiting countries overseas. The same highly skilled mechanic would go along with the car. He did so for many years. The story goes that on return from an overseas visit, the Queen wished to see him. In the presence of the Queen, he received a gift of gold cufflinks for his long service accompanying the royal car.

There are many complimentary myths about Rolls Royce cars that the company would never deny, so it is said. One is that they never break down. Well, that might have been so, but one did break down with the Queen and Duke of Edinburgh in the Mall on the way to a State service at Westminster Abbey. The cause of the breakdown was a small piece of cloth in the petrol system. The last mechanic to service the car was my Australian friend. He kept his job and escaped deportation! The car breaking down is lost in the mist of time. We had a pact that I would not spread the word that it was he who was last serviced the car when it broke down in The Mall, if he would not spread the word of 'Free Wales' underneath the HRH car at the Prince Charles Investiture. We both broke the pact!

At lunchtime, I would often sit on the perimeter wall of Rolls Royce and watch the South Wales train. The boundary wall I would sit on can still be seen from the train, as it slows down to enter Paddington. It is now a large agency for used car sales. Its change of use is a monument to the demise of the UK's car industry. Decades before I went to Rolls Royce, the Bentley motorcar company had been taken over by Rolls Royce. Bentley kept its marque, but the mechanics of the car was that of Rolls Royce. BMW took responsibility for Rolls Royce in 2003. Bentley is now a division of Volkswagen.

Colleagues would remark, mockingly, that the coach-built Rolls Royce and Bentley had the longest production line in the world. Standard cars were built entirely in Crewe. Not so with the coach-built car; the chassis and mechanics were assembled in Crewe. The car then went to London, where the handmade body was attached to the car. That's efficiency for you!

Over the four years in London, I had become an expert and highly skilled on the maintenance of Rolls Royce cars. On leaving to return to Merthyr to get married the extensive knowledge and skills became instantly redundant. But I wanted to keep my extensive knowledge of Rolls Royce cars, so I did consider applying for the Rolls Royce agency in the channel island of Jersey. Yet again, however, Merthyr was unkindly calling.

To maintain an emotional link with Rolls Royce, I left £6 in their pension scheme. A few years ago, I wrote to the company to ask the value of the pension I could expect. It was £50. I accepted it. That was the end of my link with Rolls Royce. The four years I had been there was a happy period and played a significant part in what I am today.

A final remark about Rolls Royce: In the South Wales valleys, it is often said that valley people will not travel far to work; for some this is true. Well, my colleague who lived on the west side of London had never been to the centre of London, though it was only four miles away. Another odd point of interest is that he ate little more than cheese sandwiches!

8: City Life

London is a roost for every bird

Benjamin Disraeli

I desperately needed to share in a university social life, like many of my friends who had passed their 11+ examination. I was not going to university, not even as a mature student without qualifications. London provided a surrogate university social life, and I had created it while working for Rolls Royce. But there was a profound loss I felt about something; it was that I had not mastered 'stomping', the latest dance craze indulged in by university students. In Brentford pubs in West London, I would watch these students stomping but for me it was out of reach, because it seemed like it was something reserved for the university elite. Of course, university students spend their time with fellow university students. I was in London, and I was relieved to be there. I was, though, on my own for a while until I made new friends and caught up with my friends from Wales.

When not returning to Wales on weekends, house parties just appeared. I was in my mid-twenties exploring my own personality, politics and intellect. New friendship groups were formed, and these formed other friendship groups. I had three categories of friends: work friends; Welsh teaching friends and Merthyr friends who had moved to London. I also made friends with people I had met on the train, always back to London on Sunday.

I went one evening to a pub in Bayswater, one that attracted those of a professional class. It was a mild autumn evening with couples drinking outside. I sat down with my pint of beer. A group of three were standing near me, a young woman in hot pants, with a thigh gap [The term *thigh gap* didn't receive widespread news coverage until December 2012, thanks to Victoria Beckham, David Beckham's wife.] and two young men. However, it's worth a note that a preeminent historian of anatomy, specialising in the upper leg, of The Royal Academy of Dance, records that the *thigh gap* was first spotted in the early period of the 60s decade, during a performance of Swan Lake, so it is said.

How I wished I could make the group of three a group of four. Would my social background be close enough to theirs to engage in conversation? I doubt if the men were motor mechanics. There was no way I could join them. I had fallen into the pit of social unease. I climbed out of the pit and drove back to my London digs.

There was another occasion where I struggled socially during an evening with a woman my Welsh friends wanted me to meet and introduce to the West End. Looking back on the evening, I can't remember why it was suggested that I act as a tour guide. Early in the evening it soon became evident that our upbringing made conversation difficult. We met in Mayfair. Into my MG midget we went. Sitting in a West End pub together, conversation focused on The Troubles in Ireland. She took the British side; I took the side of the IRA. It was not a pleasant evening and there was not enough time to talk about anything else and make up ground from our earlier unease. We called into KFC on the way back to her flat in Mayfair. I had, after all, promised to take her for dinner in the West End. Chivalry kicked in, and she went first into the KFC *restaurant* and walked nose first into the strengthened glass door. I asked if she was fine, but I did not display sufficient sympathy for her to desire another meeting. She got out of my MG – the only thing that we might have in common, an MG – and I said good night. She leaned toward me and said, 'You may kiss me'; I accepted with my newly found social etiquette.

Notwithstanding the awkward evening, the good times in London were made even better with my car, a new royal blue MG midget. It was the late sixties, and the soundtrack was The Beatles, The Rolling Stones and The Who; a new genre of music free of social class; a type of music not connected with a cultural hinterland. On one occasion, returning from work, it was announced on Radio 1 that the new Beatles record would be played after the 5 o'clock news. In excited anticipation I waited in my car outside my digs to listen to the Beatles new release.

It was the era of Mary Quant, miniskirts and Biba. Quant's shop in Kensington, was a must visit for young women. I went there with my fiancée, who bought an attractive brown woollen jacket. Bell-bottom trousers were fashionable for young men. I saw a pair of black bell-bottom fine corduroy trousers in *The Sunday Times*. I could not wait to buy them, and I did so as soon as I could, immediately after work the next day. It was a shop in Kensington, opposite Biba; being opposite Biba gave cachet.

Decimalisation of money took place in February 1971. Before that currency consisted of pounds, shillings, and pence. Decimalisation or not, money was short. It put an endless strain on the sum I had at the end of each week when I was on a salary. I used to consider how much petrol I had left in my car when totalling up the money I had for the rest of the week. In the same week that I had three shillings a week rise in my salary, the rail fare to Cardiff went up by the same amount. Not to worry, I was having a good time. When I was flush with cash, I would come home on the new Pullman service and have dinner on the train. It was just so wonderful and close to sophistication. On one journey, the waiter asked if I'd like more French fries. I answered, 'Yes please'. That felt good. I treated myself on two occasions by travelling back on the sleeper train, then going directly to Rolls Royce.

My time in London was a new world and worth every penny, even when I was short of pennies occasionally. I had found a place to belong, though I knew it would not last, due to my obligation to return to Wales and marry. There was, however, the choice I could have made which would have provided me with a reason to stay in London rather than return to Merthyr, by becoming a student there and then, on graduation, take up a post as a teacher of Motor Vehicle Studies in London. Had I become a qualified teacher I might have made the permanent leap from Merthyr to London.

I had achieved vocational qualifications; I had the technical language of the motor industry, but I did not have the vocabulary to argue on political and societal matters about which I felt passionate. I was attracted to the term 'sociology' and began reading about the discipline. It excited me and confirmed I was not the only one talking about the causes of society's unfairness through the prism of sociology. I was acquiring the language of the discipline and it provided a gateway to answers I had been struggling with since adolescence. It gave respectability and a discourse for my left-wing politics. I was smitten. I wanted to distinguish myself from uneducated working-class behaviours and values to middle-class behaviours and values. I became self-satisfied by being selective on sociological theory and empirical evidence. I sought out texts that would allow me to confirm that I did not have working-class behaviours. I had lower-middle-class behaviours, or so I assumed.

It was a period of liberation for the post war generation, and I was in London. My only restriction was Merthyr calling. Travelling home frequently, and often in my MG midget, I felt that I was living in my car; it became an unhealthy bubble in which I was trapped. I became increasingly conflicted by the forces of life in London and life in the valleys of South Wales. I failed to fully grow socially in London. It was a passion lost.

I explored, with friends, wealthy middle-class towns of Southwest London. Richmond and Putney became favourite haunts. We explored Kingston-upon-Thames, Epsom, Barns, Wimbledon, and more. Road patterns were different from the straight terraced streets of the valleys. This I would notice driving home from a week's holiday in Bournemouth with my parents. The pubs were different; they were proudly old and had not been modernised. There were restaurants like I'd never seen before. So many cafés were populated by young people.

All towns seemed close to rivers. The bridges were more than functional; I remember the arched stone-built bridges. The street architecture featured buildings with space between them. My memory is of long front gardens with privet hedges; privet hedges provided the only similarity with Wales! All was clean and bright as I drove in the summertime in my MG midget with the top down in the Surrey towns. Surrey towns tantalised me, and they still do.

I was fascinated by Earl's Court, nicknamed Kangaroo Valley. It was where I would meet my Australian friend in the evening. It seemed that all the large Victorian houses were converted to flats where single young people, of my age, lived together. It was where I should be living. It was where I wanted to live, yet once more, I did not take the leap and leave Merthyr behind.

There were Sundays when I would visit museums and art galleries. The Science Museum in South Kensington I would visit frequently. Car parking was not a problem in those days. The Natural History Museum was within walking distance of the Science Museum. The Royal Academy of Art I would visit in Piccadilly. I would particularly enjoy a visit to the London Transport Museum in Covent Garden. If sightseeing in the West End, I often would spend a few hours in the National Portrait Gallery. I felt privileged to enjoy such well known architecture, art and experience a culture new to me.

I'm conscious of slight changes in my accent and dialect over the years, though it is undeniably *Valley*. It is mainly due to living out of Aberfan since I was twenty-three years of age. My father was a language stickler. He would correct me on 'were' and 'was', 'have' and 'has'. I'm still conscious of the correct use of these words. Moving to London exposed my dialect and accent, and some odd terms. I could hear my accent. My dialect would be characterised by phrases such as 'I'll be there now in a minute'. My most humorous moment was when a Rolls Royce friend said, 'What's 'avee'? I explained it was 'have he', though even this was meant to be 'has he'. There's little need to mention the use of '*by* here, and *by* there. One success in life was to ensure that my children would seldom say '*by*', as in '*by* there' or '*by* here.

The *Valley* accent has been reinforced over the sixty years since I was a child. I'm not sure why this is so, but I've taken it to be to do with a decline in professional occupations, combined with a decline in the number of people moving into the valleys to work in large UK and international companies. The closure of the Hoover factory is such an example.

On becoming a technician in Rolls Royce, my employment contract changed from a weekly wage to a monthly salary. The technical department was small, comprising just three men and one secretary. The working culture and atmosphere were so different from being a mechanic on the workshop floor. There was a shortage of fun, charisma and conversation outside of tasks and procedures. My radical left-wing politics was anathema to the office, apart from the Southern Ireland secretary.

70

As mechanics, we all knew what each of us was earning. The wage had an incremental scale with criteria for progressing up the wage scale. No one knew the salary of colleagues in the technical department, and no one dared ask. My pay was fixed, with no extra payment for overtime, whereas when I was a mechanic, I could increase my take-home pay by working overtime. Being able to top up my wage came in handy. I earned less as a technician than as a mechanic, but that was the cost of status, which is rather sad really. Wages increased with the cost of living annually but not salaries. Nothing changed there then.

I devised a way of reducing the cost of travelling home by train by using the return ticket more than once. At the time, return rail tickets were valid for three months – they are now valid for one month. It could only be done on the homeward journey. Automatic barriers to enter and exit platforms did not exist. Therefore, each train had a ticket collector, whose job it was to validate a ticket by punching a hole in it. It was noticed after a while that the ticket collector would begin checking tickets through the train at the London end and would have validated tickets by the first stop in Reading, thirty minutes later. The clever strategy was to sit in the front half of the train until Reading. Knowing that the ticket collector had completed the rear half of the train by Reading, you would then move to a seat where the ticket collector had completed punching tickets in the rear coaches. There were a few exceptions to this, such as when the ticket collector returned to the rear end of the train to validate tickets of passengers who had joined the train at stations along the route to Cardiff. There would always be a valid ticket, but the strategy was to avoid it being punched by the ticket collector.

Going west the M4 ended at Reading. On one occasion the traffic came to a stop, and after a while it moved slowly. The reason for the hold-up became clear a few slow miles towards Reading. It was a serious accident on the London bound carriageway. I looked across and there was what looked like a body. I felt that I had no right to witness this. I was disturbed by the thought that I had no right to see the body before the family did.

71

9: Education Education Education

We all have two lives. The second one starts when we realise we only have one.

Confucius

I returned to Merthyr and married. My wife was a Catholic, albeit lapsed. I knew my parents were not happy with this, though never said so; Baptists and Catholics would never share a pavement in the valleys. Each was ignorant of each other's faith.

I took a temporary teaching job at Merthyr Tydfil College of Further Education, teaching apprentice motor mechanics. The college motor vehicle section's teachers kept themselves apart from the rest of the engineering department, and therefore the rest of the college. The staff room of the motor vehicle section was a converted corridor; that was the choice of the existing motor vehicle teachers. There was little room for me to do lesson preparation in a corridor, and not much enthusiasm to create space for a newcomer.

The welcome and induction was so different from Rolls Royce, where new colleagues were readily accepted.

I was primarily to blame for being unable to manage the cultural shock of living in a London life in a valley town. I would use the college main staff room during lunchtimes and engage with engineers, English teachers, business studies teachers, have coffee and talk about all manner of topics. It only served to reinforce my unhappiness at not allowing myself to be accepted by the team of motor vehicle teachers. Nevertheless, teaching was an exciting change of direction. When I became a motor vehicle apprentice, I enjoyed much of the work, especially in Rolls Royce, but engineering was never going to be a fulfilling career.

An opportunity arose for me to change departments from Motor Vehicle Studies to the department where Liberal Studies was taught. It came with much joy when I eventually left the motor vehicle section and joined the business and general education department. There I taught Liberal Studies, Communication Studies and eventually on teacher education courses. By this time, I had gained a university PGCE teaching qualification. I had found my vocation; I was completely at ease with teacher education, and I retain an interest to this day.

There was a crossover for a while where I continued to teach Liberal Studies to the students who knew me from teaching Motor VehicleS. They considered me as *one of them*; I spoke their language; we had shared some experiences. Liberal studies, taught by a teacher who had been a motor mechanic, gave the subject a relevance to their lives.

With the beginning of the next academic year, I taught Liberal Studies to new first year motor vehicle students, who saw me solely as a Liberal Studies teacher who had no idea what it was like to be a motor vehicle apprentice. The student-teacher dynamic had changed; my relations with the students, and theirs with me, was completely different. Without the shared connection of the motor industry, teaching Liberal Studies to students who were in college to become skilled motor mechanics, made the teaching of Liberal Studies much more demanding than hitherto. I did continue to speak in a quiet teacher's voice, however, relying on the theory that if I spoke quietly, so would the students. It was not an entirely successful theory, with young men's testosterone overflowing, but it worked more often than not.

My teaching timetable included teaching Communication Studies to adults returning to employment. Up to this period I had only taught young people, most of whom were apprentices, and it could be assumed that their life experiences were not too dissimilar from each other; for instance, they would all have recently left school. Consequently, lesson planning would be pitched to enable all to reach the lesson objectives. This was not the case with adults. Adult classes would include students with a variety of backgrounds, educational achievements, and career aspirations. Lesson preparation for these classes was much more difficult than for teaching apprentices. Lessons had to be designed to engage adults with a wide range of motivations and abilities. Teaching was challenging and on occasion unnerving. One of the most unsettling issues was trying to confidently assess if each student was grasping the objectives of the lesson. When teaching apprentices, it is not too difficult to interpret each student's understanding of a topic by their behaviour, by their facial expressions and by their questions. With adults, the interpretation of students' understanding of lesson content is much more difficult to ascertain; a *pensive* facial expression can be the same as a *vacant* facial expression. Selective questioning, debate and discussion will help a class of adults, with a range of life experiences, to achieve the lesson objectives, one hopes.

All colleges in the South Wales valleys were primarily created to train those employed in collieries. All towns and a few large villages had their college. Mining and engineering departments had more day-release apprentices than all other departments together. Mining apprentices were the apprentice kings, way above bricklaying apprentices, electrical apprentices and carpentry apprentices. They were better paid than other apprentice trades. Therefore, they could afford to go on an educational visit to London for the day, as they wished to do. With less mature or younger apprentices, such education visits were highly structured and organised. It was not necessary with the class of mining apprentices. They had the freedom of London, with just one stipulation: that they would all be back at Paddington station for the journey home. On one trip seventeen in the class left Merthyr College in the coach to Cardiff, to take the new 125 fast train to London. Sixteen were at Paddington for the designated train home. Seventeen up sixteen back. Something was wrong. Where was the missing student? Who would tell his parents that he did not catch the train and why he was not at Paddington? I've no idea what one of his fellow students might have said to his parents that evening, or when he got home the following day. But the reason he did not catch the train was because he had a good night's sleep in Bow Street police station. No one ever told the whole story, but we all know that whatever happened, it happened in Soho.

Thankfully, not all Liberal Studies events ended the lesson with one student less at the end of the lesson than the beginning. Three lesson topics would always generate interest and debate: George Orwell's *Animal Farm*, 'Give Peace a Chance', by John Lennon, and an international rugby question about Wales playing England, 'Do you want Wales to win or England to lose?'

Shortly after gaining my in-service teaching qualification at Cardiff University, and beginning my bachelor's degree, the director of the PGCE course at Cardiff University offered me a secondment, to tutor on the course I had a year earlier studied as a student. The principal of Merthyr Tydfil College eventually acceded to my request to accept the secondment for two periods, covering one year. It was through the secondment to university that I knew, for the first time in my life, that I stood out from the crowd, and it was as an educator.

A while later, on return from secondment to the department of Business Studies, I became concerned about the favourable teaching timetable the Head of Department was giving to his wife. Boldly, or rashly perhaps, I convened a meeting of all teachers in the department of business studies and invited the Head of Department to the meeting to ask why he was giving his wife, who was on a part-time contract, a teaching timetable convenient to her, consequently meaning that some full-time teaching staff had timetables requiring them to have a long day.

Over the nine years I was at Merthyr College almost all senior management appointments went to external candidates. Councillors on the appointment boards were ignorant of the demoralising effect the policy of favouring external candidates had on college staff. Such a policy over such a long period led to the phenomenon of *revenge theory*. Some teachers lost the drive to develop new courses, though the quality of teaching did not suffer.

I was introduced to the Socratic teaching methodology while on the PGCE. I was attracted to this method of teaching, and where appropriate I would use it to fully engage students throughout my time at Merthyr Tydfil College. Rather naively, when new in post as vice-principal of Pontypridd College, I used the Socratic approach when consulting a group of teachers about changes to the organisation of the college. No sooner had I invited teachers for their view on my tentative proposal, when one in the group rather abruptly said, 'Why are you asking for our view? You should know, you are the new vice-principal!

Several years later I invited him to join one of my working groups

75

to draft a potentially contentious policy. I asked him to join the working group because of his cynicism; not that he knew that. I had the view that if *he* supported the policy, he would not obstruct the policy's implementation; it worked a treat, and he became a strong advocate of the policy amongst colleagues. I would occasionally invite cynics onto other working groups on the same basis, hoping that they would champion the implementation of new working practices.

While on secondment to Cardiff University, I wrote a letter to an academic journal on research apropos further and higher education. The letter expressed my concern that there were those in FE colleges - usually managers – who would speak at conferences in glowing terms about their college. The presentation may be a passing take on what was going on in their college, or what they wanted conference to think what was going on in their college. I referred to those conference speakers as *phantom curriculum experts*. I included the letter with my application details to the Further Education and Curriculum Review Development Unit; often referred to as FEU. I believe that my letter was a significant factor that led to me being shortlisted and subsequently appointed to FEU as a development officer, on secondment.

I was so delighted to be shortlisted. The appointment panel of four was in stark contrast to the large interview panels I was familiar with in South Wales. It was more an exploration, discussion and probing regarding the purpose of FEU in supporting the FE sector to cope with a worrying rise in unemployment amongst the young. The four on the interview panel were the FEU director, the personnel officer, and two senior civil servants from the Department of Education and Science. My CV revealed that my first qualification was not until six years after leaving school, and that this was a vocational education qualification.

I had by now a first-class degree and considerable experience of teaching the young unemployed. I also fully understood the nature of the curriculum that would engage those who had not done well in school. It was not too far off from my own experience of education in a secondary modern school, and therefore, I suppose my empathy came through during the interview. One panel member politely questioned my absence of qualifications since leaving school. 'What were you doing over that six-year period after leaving school?' To which I replied, 'Well, I have been living throughout the period'. The panel chortled at my retort. I would never have made such a remark at an interview panel in South Wales. Chortles are rare emotions with interview panels in South Wales.

Later, I caught the train back to Cardiff, wondering what the panel thought of me. I thought I had not impressed the panel. I consoled myself that at least I interviewed well, but the relevance of my contribution to the panel was another thing, so nothing was lost, and it was good experience at being interviewed by a panel of professionals.

I opened the post the following morning, and to my amazement, with a trembling shock, I was offered the seconded position of FEU Development Officer. My salary was higher than as a senior lecturer at Merthyr Tydfil College. I learned later that my salary caused consternation with longer serving civil servants. There were just three development officers, and we were not strictly civil servants, but persons appointed for our professional expertise. We were on short term contracts; a turnover of short-term appointments was intended to ensure the FEU remained fresh with new ideas for curriculum design and advice on implementation of new courses. It is a lesson that Colleges Wales, a membership organisation to support FE colleges in Wales, should learn.

I joined FEU in September 1980 and returned to University College, Cardiff eighteen months later. It was intended to be a three-year secondment, but due to the strain of a demanding job and family it was agreed that I could end my contract. My FEU office looked across the River Thames to Greater London County Hall. The view never did threaten my imposter syndrome! The FEU was created by government, located in London, as an 'intelligence' agency to develop curricula for unemployed young people as a preparation for employment. It was a small unit. The further education sector considered FEU to be at the cutting edge of curriculum development. On leaving the unit halfway through my secondment I could have taken the easy option of returning to Merthyr College, but I considered that this would be a

77

backward career step. I took a chance and returned to the Education Faculty of Cardiff University on a one-year contract. It became a rolling contract for five years until I became vice-principal at Pontypridd College, where I stayed for twenty years, with the college merging with three local colleges to become the second largest FE college in Wales.

During my time at Cardiff, I ran a special unit for training instructors involved with unemployed young people.

It was a period of seminal curriculum development. Several government reports provided the policy framework to advise the FE sector. One such programme designed to prepare disadvantaged youths was the Youth Opportunities Programme. The chair of the design group was Geoffrey Holland, a senior civil servant. As is common in the UK, official reports are referred to by the surname of the reporter's chair. In this case, it was referred to as the Holland Report. A friend who was a senior education officer in a North Wales local education authority related the humorous case of the report when summarised in Welsh for the education committee. The Holland Report was translated as the 'Netherlands Report'. The error was corrected just in time.

It was so refreshing to work with a small group of colleagues involved in such significant curriculum development and research in response to the government's social and employment policies to reduce the unemployment rate of young people.

I lived during the week with a friend from Merthyr in her Paddington flat. I would spend most evenings together with her friends in a pub. I was a little uneasy with this, owing to having a family in Merthyr. I was conflicted, yet again, but I needed to bear the difficult circumstances in the interest of my career. We'd arranged to meet for drinks after work, and that she would phone where we were to meet. She had my work phone number at the Department of Education and Science, or DES. She did not know that this was an acronym, and she asked the operator to put her through to Des!

Another humorous event was when I was waiting in a pub near Shrewsbury on my way to Mid Wales for a conference the following day. It was late evening as I was waiting, and my eyes were blurred after a busy day from a presentation in Birmingham. I was sitting in the corner of the pub with a pint of beer on the table. After a while I noticed that an attractive middle-aged woman kept on looking at me. It was slightly beyond a flattering stare of hers, to the point that I didn't know where to rest my eyes. Five minutes before the train was due, I got up to leave, and I turned back to the table to pick up my pint glass and take it back to the bar. There I was standing with my back to the woman, and I glanced up to see *EastEnders* on the television above my head. I smiled at the women on leaving, but her eyes had been glued to *EastEnders* and not me for the last twenty minutes.

The FEU director would provide the four development officers with a specific work schedule, which we were required to interpret in meeting objectives. There was also a regional responsibility for disseminating the work of the unit and curriculum research. I covered Wales and the West Country and the unit's objective of advising on Basic Skills. A section I wrote on teaching transferable skills related to Basic Skills is included in the textbook *Teaching and Learning in Further and Adult Education*, (Longman 2002). Further, I have been cited in several other publications and contributed to many publications on further education.

Proofreading research projects for publication was part of my work. One such research project was to reveal the poor literacy skills of FE teachers who mainly taught practical skills in college workshops. One chapter was included to show the errors vocational teachers made in their worksheets for students and apprentices. The chapter had so many errors to correct that I referred the corrected text to the researcher for the last check prior to publication. To the dismay of the researcher, the examples he used to show the low level of literacy of vocational teachers had been corrected by me! Had the error not been corrected at the final stage for publication it would have completely undermined the project's purpose. Much of the research subsequently informed the FEU *Basic Skills* publication, which I drafted.

A project manager and his team from Sussex University had developed a curriculum framework that, if accepted by vocational education qualification agencies, would be radically different to existing vocational courses. The distinguished project manager asked to meet with me in a London hotel to brief me on the curriculum framework and asked if I would consider mentioning it at relevant policy groups. There followed a further meeting with prominent vocational education experts to agree a strategy to promote the curriculum framework. In the event the strategy failed and the framework was never implemented. It did though give me an insight into a form of lobbying to influence policy; curriculum policy in this case.

I went on a two-week study tour with a group of senior college managers to Germany. The purpose of the tour was to learn about the German apprenticeship system. The tour was well organised, with study group meetings of senior policymakers, skilled vocational teachers, and apprentices. We flew out and then travelled by train from city to city. We went to colleges and training centres, guided by government personnel. The cities we visited were Munich, Düsseldorf, Frankfurt, and Berlin. There were times after long days and long train journeys when we would be exhausted. On one occasion we checked into our hotel in Berlin and were escorted to our rooms. Settling into my room, I placed my tour file on the bedside table. As usual, there were leaflets and books for visitors. I perused a couple, and one caught my eye, and there it was, a poor translation giving visitors helpful information that included Berlin's location, emphasising the City's accessibility, it read, 'Berlin isn't far from anywhere'. There are not many cities in the world that are not far from anywhere – lucky Berlin denizens!

10: Returning to Cardiff University

I never let schooling get in the way of my education

Mark Twain

W hen I returned to Cardiff University, I quickly settled into the faculty because of my earlier secondment. I knew all the lecturers.

In the early years of the 1970s University College, Cardiff, created a Department of Further Education. The cadre of about ten lecturers was taken on together to develop teacher education qualifications for FE teachers. In the early years of the new department hundreds of in-service further education lecturers gained their PGCE. There were also PGCE students who were pre-employment in further education.

The Department of Further Education was innovative, relevant and of high quality for the first ten years or so. But it began to fail, becoming stale and out of touch with the changes that were taking place in further education colleges. The initial cadre of the department's lecturers grew old together. A few lecturers turned to an increasing style of pontificating, compounded by a loss of empathy. The creation and demise of the Further Education Department provides a classic case of what happens to organisations, including university departments and further education colleges, if new, and essentially younger, employees are not recruited in order to ensure the organisation remains relevant.

On leaving to become a vice-principal, only one new lecturer had joined the team of lecturers. At 40 years of age, I was the youngest lecturer on the course.

Eventually, the PGCE became a shadow of itself, and due to other programmes for getting an FE teaching qualification, the course closed.

The conclusion of a survey by the (former) Institute of Personnel Management of the age profile of FE college teachers found that colleges were suffering from 'middle-age spread'; consequently, there were not enough young teachers with up-to-date vocational knowledge, practices, and skills in FE colleges.

Earlier, as an undergraduate student in the Department of Education, I experienced the poor teaching quality of a couple of lecturers as the department became moribund. My tutorial group, at the instigation of the lecturer, was considering the changing demography of college enrolments. A contribution I made related to the turndown in the economy having a knock-on effect on opportunities for social mobility of well qualified further education students. The lecturer replied by interpreting social *mobility* as geographic *relocation* for employment.

Teaching at Cardiff University, my specialism was 'New curricula in vocational preparation for the young unemployed.' My four years in the Education Faculty of Cardiff University were stimulating and enjoyable. I had done the course I was now teaching on twelve years earlier while teaching at Merthyr college.

It was the time when the Education Department enrolled many hundreds of students from Nigeria, funded by the oil boom. Their three year degree course in education studies included a ten thousand word dissertation. If the title of a dissertation included the word *technology* or *engineering* there was a good chance that I would be their dissertation supervisor. There was one adult student who struggled more than most with the English language. I would see him weekly to review his progress. Over an extended period, there were occasions when I would be correcting my own work! He achieved a pass degree and went on his way back to a senior job in Lagos. He wrote to me to thank me for my support and detailing the position he had on his return. Needless to say, the letter was written in English, or close enough to English, for me to get the drift of his gratitude for the time and support I gave him in ensuring his dissertation was accepted as a pass by the external examiner. I was pleased with my result!

The PGCE course included a weekend residential programme. The residential venue was in the coastal village of Aberthaw. The main employer was Aberthaw Cement. The village was dusted with dry cement. While having breakfast on the first morning one of the adult students uttered, 'I was woken up by sparrows coughing'.

11: Vice Principal Appointment

Before I speak, I have something important to say

Groucho Marx

I 've already mentioned that I was teaching on the Further Education PGCE course at University College Cardiff, on an annual rolling contract, when I applied for the post of vice principal at Pontypridd College. I was one of six shortlisted candidates; one of whom was a senior careers officer, employed by the county. As an insider, he expected to get the job. My turn came: ten minutes to read three questions, and then shortly afterwards I was led into the county hall debating chamber. I was introduced to the panel by the chairman (all members of the appointment committee were men - nothing new there then) and told that I had ten minutes to answer the three questions, and that I must not go over the ten minutes. Ten minutes for a senior management post! I looked around the council chamber. It was not too dissimilar from the seating arrangement of an old-fashioned classroom.

I decided there and then that I would answer each question as if I was teaching a lesson (a very short lesson!). I anticipated what the first question would be, and it was what I expected: 'Will you please tell us why you want the job and how your experience and qualifications equip you for the job.' In my mind I thought I had no more than three minutes to answer this, leaving seven minutes to convince the appointment committee that I should have the post. I answered the first question and could see a *low yawning rate*. I would warn my PGCE students to look out for the class of students' *yawning rate* when on teaching practice. If more than fifty percent of the students yawn, you were failing to maintain their interest.

I had seven minutes left to answer the remaining two questions, both on leadership and management. Who on earth wrote such daft questions, I thought? Well, neither question was difficult to answer; I simply spoke to each question as if I was summarising the key points of a lesson; a technique, again, I would recommend to my university students. I could tell by the low amount of fidgeting and the low yawning rate that it was a successful lesson. Shortly afterwards, I was invited back into the council chamber and offered the post. The rush of high emotion is one I had never experienced; it was close to being informed by FEU that I had been offered the post of Development Officer. This was my reward for long periods of focused determination, reinforced with years of studying.

I learned later that they wanted new blood for the appointment of vice-principal. I was forty-one, the youngest vice principal in Wales, and there I stayed for twenty years overseeing the merger of two colleges and an art centre into Pontypridd College. It was, for almost every moment, a most enjoyable time, especially with my high profile in the further education sector in Wales. I worked well with colleagues, helping them to develop quality courses, new teaching methodologies and encouragement to innovate.

It was getting the post of Vice-Principal that gave me a good reason to move south of South Wales. Pontypridd College is fifteen miles south of where we were living in Merthyr. This was the opportunity I had longed for to leave Merthyr. We looked at houses in Cowbridge but it was not to be. My wife would not move from Merthyr. It was years later that I would leave Merthyr to a village near Cardiff with a new partner, whom I subsequently married.

As Vice-Principal I was the senior manager accountable for the quality of courses and strategic planning, all in consultation with colleagues. Even though my position was senior, with concomitant legal authority, I led on the principle of rational authority, acknowledging that good management is a precondition of good leadership. My intention was always to lead alongside colleagues, with an objective that would be refined in consultation, usually with teaching teams who knew I respected their expertise and specialist subject knowledge.

It remained that way for the whole of my twenty years as Vice-Principal. I would exercise strong influence over policy but seldom usurped my authority. Those curriculum areas that required little intervention, and therefore light-touch management, were the most successful in winning national awards and the highest grades when assessed by HMI inspectors.

I was alert to the difference between *interfering* in decisions made by professional teachers, and *intervening* to agree solutions, or unobtrusive monitoring. I would try to never impose a decision not shared with colleagues; though I would engage in argument, as ought to happen in a dynamic and innovative organisation. This approach was confirmed in an HMI inspection report on the college that, '*The principal and vice-principal provide competent and unobtrusive leadership.*'

The way I related to teachers allowed me to listen, support and encourage innovation with individuals and amongst teaching teams. It is for managers and senior teachers to create the right environment to support teachers to continue to care for their students. Some colleagues would prefer to be directed in their work; others would like to make their own decisions, usually within a team. Teams of teachers who work with minimum supervision would know the boundaries of their decision-making responsibilities and would consult with me only if the issue was exceptional, or required significant additional resources, including increasing members of the teaching team.

Gradually I promoted, with colleagues, the adoption of *distributed management* as a form of leadership. The essence of distributed management is that teams of teachers are accountable for their own decisions in relation to quality of courses, students' learning, and meeting needs of employers.

Inevitably, not all teaching teams, or individuals within a team, are willing or sufficiently confident to accept the responsibilities of managing courses within their curriculum area. None of this is to say that there were not intractable views from time to time. A period of time and critical reflection may overcome intractable views. Continuing intransigence of an individual may require the intervention of a personnel manager. A programme of professional development may need to be arranged for a teacher who continually underperforms. Peers may address underperforming teachers without the intervention of management. Personal issues, perhaps illness, relationship issues or family concerns, a colleague may wish to share with a confidant, who

85

might be a manager or close colleague.

An inevitability of our education system is that a time will come when colleges will be visited by HMI. Such visits are not always a pleasant experience because from the day you know the inspectors are coming the college is under a constant cloud of anxiety. Daily life is absorbed by trying to put in place all the things the inspectors are looking for which would otherwise be neglected by even the most conscientious employee. The miracle of an impending inspection, however, is that senior management can suddenly conjure up the finance to provide many of the resources that staff have been crying out for since the last inspection. The downside is that when the new resources arrive days beforehand, the staff sometimes have no clue how to use the equipment. The Estates Manager may finally get his act into gear, toilets may get a deep clean, repair jobs are suddenly completed and the smell of fresh paint will gradually percolate the corridors and classrooms as the fearful day approaches.

Managers spend inordinate hours briefing staff, both teaching and administrative, confident that their pep talks will do the trick and turn under-performing areas into outstanding provision in a matter of weeks. Files that haven't been used for months, if not years, suddenly become populated with mountains of paperwork in an attempt to show how good we all are.

Finally, the dreaded day arrives. Most lecturers perform heroically, doing their best to pull out all the stops. Some will churn out their *one* decent lesson and be encouraged by the positive comments from HMI about the lesson observations. Others will try to impress and do something in class they have never attempted before and be disappointed when the students are completely bemused. A few will phone in feigning illness, sudden deaths of family members, or simply not turn up hoping it will all go away. It is not unknown for some teachers to teach the same lesson a week before the inspection to the same students. Unwittingly, teachers using this trick usually fall foul of students' inevitable lack of spontaneity; a vital element in lessons taught by good engaging teachers.

An inspector gave one lecturer some good advice after he delivered his grade 1 lesson during an inspection. Many outstanding features of the lesson were reported and only one shortcoming was offered for consideration for future lessons. 'Buy new shoes,' the inspector said, 'The ones you're wearing click as you walk around the laboratory and clearly distract learners' concentration.' It might seem sound and encouraging advice. Fortunately, the clicking wasn't so loud that it kept the inspector awake for the whole duration of the lesson! It was well known that the inspector had narcolepsy.

As vice-principal I would meet middle managers on the first Friday of each month. There were about fifteen middle managers, each responsible for a curriculum area. The meetings became a most effective and supportive way of exchanging ideas, consulting on curriculum matters and announcing policies, including Welsh Assembly policies. Often, topics would be led by colleagues, or visiting experts. The morning meeting would end with a buffet. The meeting would rotate across three campuses. One college was deep in the Rhondda valley, one was located in Pontypridd at the foot of four South Wales valleys, and the other was close to Cardiff. Each campus would put on a buffet in turn. The thickness of the buffet sandwiches was in keeping with the socio-economic community of the campus. Rhondda campus had the thickest sandwiches, with white bread. Pontypridd campus had sandwiches of regular thickness, brown and white bread. The campus that was close to Cardiff, which was the college's business centre, had brown and white dainty sandwiches, without crusts!

From 1992, for posts below senior management, interview panels would be chaired by the principal or me. As a panel chair, I would create the conditions of my interview at FEU. I would, though, be aware of the dangers of cloning in acknowledging the behaviours and strengths of interviewees. There are serious risks to the dynamic of the college in being overly influenced by making cloning appointments. Notwithstanding this, where I witnessed behaviours of hesitancy and seeming lack of confidence, I was aware that they might be an indication of the interviewee being cautious in communicating to the panel what might actually be a considered view.

I would seek agreement with members of the panel on who should be appointed. If the favoured candidate declined to accept the offer to be employed at the college, I would recommend that it should *not* be offered to the second-best candidate. The second-best candidate is just that, second best. When that happened, my advice to the interview panel would be to advertise the post again.

There were times though, when the panel could not agree on who was the most suitable candidate because the merits of each were so close. When this happened, I would adjourn the interview panel until the following morning. There were times when the relative qualities of an interviewee would be for panel members to argue their case for their preferred candidate. There were cases where I would favour an internal candidate if there was a fine judgement to be made between two candidates. Appointing an internal candidate in preference to an external candidate, when both are equally ranked, provides a signal within the organisation that there are opportunities for promotion from within the college, and that the person's capacity to meet the job specification compares favourably with external candidates.

I led administrative changes. I introduced the use of first names with colleagues. Prior to the change, senior colleagues were referred to by their job title. I changed the heading 'Christian Name' on student enrolment forms to 'First Name'. The change was resisted by the senior administrator.

There was a period during the mid-80s when colleges of further education expanded. By 1991 I had been Vice-Principal for five years and started looking for principal appointments in South Wales. I was shortlisted for two Principal posts but was not appointed. For a while, no further principalships came available in South Wales. And I never wanted to figure on the 'principal chasing circuit', which if successful would have meant a move from South Wales. It was another case of Merthyr calling. There is another reason, which was to do with my capacity to manage a college, with all its demands and complexity. My successful career was that of strategic curriculum management. I had limitations with financial management and, as an instance, I was not interested in the college estate. Though I was interested in the learning environment, such classroom layout or arrangements in workshops for apprentices.

Having a vocation has an upside and downside. It is all-consuming, with a consequent unhealthy influence on one's life caused by not spending more time with family. The upside of a vocation is the commitment and satisfaction of serving the comprehensive needs of further education.

As I matured as a vice-principal my profile increased in Wales' further education sector. It led to many invitations to chair senior meetings and conferences. I always enjoyed such events, and it was helpful that I was adept at contributing collegially to tentative or settled solutions at meetings.

In the case of the newly merged college where I was vice-principal there were courses for students:

- with special needs; physical and sensory impairments, and those with learning difficulties
- with low levels of literacy and numeracy
- learning English as a second language
- on shared courses with local secondary schools
- on general education programmes
- on vocational education programmes, including apprenticeships
- on courses in local communities
- on pre-degree courses and full degree courses
- tailored courses for employing organisations

The number of students on each course is determined by the socioeconomic profile of the region; by the nature of employment in regional industries, and by the proportion of students taking GCSE and A level courses for application to university. Most students, whatever course they were on, lived in the South Wales valleys. There were three main forms of attendance: full-time, one day a week and evening only.

My college was exceptional in the range and quality of its community courses, including courses for those with special needs and learning difficulties, where students needed to improve their ability to read, write and practise arithmetic. The college was awarded the highest grade by inspectors for these curriculum areas.

At sixty years of age, I became eligible for free bus travel, so I would take the bus to college. Each morning there would only be a few passengers, and after a while I got to know some. We would talk about work, holidays, retirement and so on. I also would get to know some drivers. Twice I left items on the bus, first, my flat cap – Welshmen are very fond of their flat caps, (Dai caps as they are often called by valley men!) – and then my wallet. I contacted the bus company, and within hours the driver of the return bus brought my items into college. In each case my bus travel acquaintances had told the drivers that I worked at Pontypridd College. Frequently a passenger and driver who knew each other would have a discussion down the bus. Other passengers would often hear these conversations. Sometimes they would be about intimate matters. One discussion was about a mutual friend who had been rushed into hospital and placed in a mixed ward of women and men. The conversation centred on the friend's shock and unease about sharing a bed with women – well, that's what we all heard. Mixed hospital wards were routine up until 2012, when they were phased out because the protection of people's privacy had become a political issue.

On getting the bus home, I would alight one stop from the terminal at Cardiff Central station. At the time the UK government had recently implemented an immigration policy for citizens of EU member states. Many needed to learn English to gain employment. The college put on flexible attendance English Language classes for those seeking work, most of whom were from Eastern European states. One local bus company enticed the immigrants to be employed as drivers. The company had a reputation for paying drivers the minimum wage, with the minimum amount of training.

As well as being economical about wages the company was economical about route knowledge, which was not sufficient to cover the detail of some routes. On one occasion, on leaving college late in the afternoon, the bus stopped and on I got, passing the driver as I showed my senior's bus pass. The driver very politely said, 'Thank you', with his accent revealing that he was from an Eastern European country. I sat down, and immediately the bus turned left. I shouted down the bus, 'This is the wrong way'. I told him which way to go, and he thanked me. The bus route follows secondary roads to Cardiff, and at certain points, he would ask which way to go through the many villages. I was by now standing directly behind him giving directions. I moved to get off the bus, which is one bus stop before the end of the bus route. Just as I was alighting, he asked anxiously, 'Which is the way to the final stop?' I explained to him that the terminus was just under a mile, and that he should turn left at the second left, right at the next turning, and left into Cardiff bus station. His eyes just rolled. I assured myself that he seemed to know how to get to the final stop. On saying goodbye, I spoke to him as I would speak to my son. I said, 'Will you be alright now? 'Yes, thank you!'

Later, in my retirement, a former colleague emailed to mention that I was on a student's Facebook page, pictured standing at the bus stop waiting for the bus home. The title of the page was 'Old man-eating orange'.

I was diligent throughout my two careers. In Rolls-Royce it involved working efficiently to specified standards. As Vice-Principal standards were related to the quality of teaching and a subject's relevance. There would be success criteria for pupils with special needs to pupils on degree courses. Each is different but achieving a specified high standard requires a professional commitment of the same order. I was a stickler with the presentation of reports of all kinds, often to an unreasonable extent. To my shame, I did not cover my impatience well with my PA, occasionally. Now that I'm retired, I seldom become impatient. Colleagues knew that I expected agreed standards to be met, and if reasonable, allowed the benefit of doubt when standards fell below expectations. My approach to leadership would be to trust colleagues to administer, develop and teach within boundaries agreed together.

In all my posts in education I would work to the boundaries of my ability. It would bring sublime satisfaction and contribute to my profile in the FE sector as someone who understood curriculum development. My understanding of strategic curriculum management was confirmed by my being asked to lecture on the topic for the MA programme for in-service college managers over the ten years of its duration.

My career in education became my spiritual home and I flourished in it. The heavy demands and responsibilities I took in my stride. Though, of course, there were some tough times. The toughest of times concerned a couple of middle managers who had been appointed through nepotism before I was in post. They were lowly qualified, hostile to innovation and devoid of strategic management skills and skills of personnel management. This was a period when the government expected colleges to collaborate much more with industry. These two cases serve to illustrate the problem of poor management in not having the experience, or propensity, of engaging with senior personnel in companies in the private and public sectors.

I had worked over a period of years to develop a partnership with the two local Welsh language comprehensive schools; one of which was adjacent to the college. The comprehensive schools needed reassurance that we would respect the Welsh language and culture, especially in the practical trades. This was difficult for the college due to the paucity of Welsh speaking skilled persons. Eventually a meeting was arranged with senior staff of the schools and Pontypridd College. While we were all settling down prior to the meeting, our Head of Construction said to one of the schoolteachers, 'Will you say something in Welsh for me?' The rapid retort was, 'Certainly not. What do you think I am, a parrot?'

The second example of collaboration involved the Head of Communication Studies; a nepotistic appointment, with subsequent serious morale problems with teachers. One of the teachers of Management Studies reminded us of 'revenge theory', a point I made earlier. For months our employment liaison officer had been in discussion with the Head of Personnel in the NHS to agree a training programme in communications with patients. The time for the meeting was arranged with the NHS personnel officer, who went on to introduce himself to the Head of Communications Studies with a not too untypical friendly remark, 'Pleased to meet you, my darling'. Her reaction to 'darling' ended all further discussion on a communication training programme. The Head of Communication Studies was from England and was ignorant of informal forms of introductions by Welsh men. It is, of course, a familiar salutation in Wales. I have gone through life being thanked at a supermarket checkout with, 'Thank you, sweetheart'.

Among the most significant transformations colleges went through when they escaped from local authority control was greater independence for the complete management of all aspects of a college. When under local education authority control, a college governing body was dominated by local authority councillors with a token employer and staff members. Governors are unpaid, though they claim expenses, and they generally provide wise advice to senior college managers on finance, estate, personnel, strategic direction, and are a touchstone on community matters. Sometimes their role is less likely to impress, however.

In the final days of local authority control a college's board of governors still consisted almost entirely of elected members of local and county councils. To assist the chairman of the board, it was usual for the principal to write the script for the chairman to introduce public meetings. At one public meeting – Annual Prize Giving - the principal inadvertently omitted to provide headings on the chairman's briefing note. The chairman, who had been given the written note just before taking his place at centre stage, proceeded to introduce the programme and then continued to thank everybody for coming and wishing them a safe journey home. To compound the error the chairman thanked the guest for the address when he was meant to introduce him. Fortunately, all guests stayed until all the students had received their prizes and the principal had given his annual address. Remarkably and thankfully, the chairman remained completely unaware of the error.

At another prize giving ceremony in the early 1980s an old valve amplifier was used to improve the volume of the public address system. All seemed to be going well with guests hearing every word from the platform speakers, but rather unfortunately they soon began to hear the wireless conversation of the taxi driver who had just arrived to take the Town Mayor home after the event. The taxi driver continued to receive messages for his next passenger from mission control. Embarrassingly the old amplifier picked up anything and everything transmitted within 200 metres and was never used again. The Town Mayor's consort left early to shut the driver up.

A frequent role for governing board members is to form the interview panel for appointments - an interview panel close on twenty members – usually all men. It was not unknown for senior college managers not to have any say in who is appointed for teaching and middle-management posts. Elected members (councillors) were seldom inhibited by nepotism; indeed, it is not a secret that an applicant's postcode carried more weight than a candidate's professional qualifications. These councillors were often confused by issues that they previously had not encountered. One such case in the late 1980s was when a promotion came up for a senior lecturer; a post which occurred infrequently. Teaching appointments and middle management posts were more frequent. Teaching interviews are allocated five minutes, with a five-minute period allowed for the candidate to read three questions. Ten minutes are allocated, again for three questions, for middle management appointments.

In the hierarchy of college posts, senior lecturers (senior teaching post with some management), are between teachers and middle management. The senior lecturer post rarity caused a problem of equity about how many minutes should be given for each candidate. After a lengthy discussion amongst the governors - I was the senior officer - they settled on seven and half minutes for each candidate. A fair settlement: seven and half minutes is equal time between five minutes for teachers and ten minutes for middle managers! In another case we needed to increase the number of Welsh-speaking teachers in specific vocational subjects. Health and Social Care was one subject, due to an increasing number of older people in residential care homes with Welsh as their first language. There were few applicants for the teaching post, but it was necessary to ensure that shortlisted applicants' Welsh was sufficiently fluent for teaching in Welsh. Only two were shortlisted. Before the formal stage of the interview, the appointment board chairman tried to put the female applicants at ease and said to each candidate, 'I could do with some caring myself''. Not one of the board members looked embarrassed by the remark. I was the senior officer at the interviews to hear this. Many years later I married the successful applicant.

The first time we met after her appointment was in the photocopy room, where my elbow bumped into her left breast. She was wearing a brown polo neck jumper and a long floral skirt. Her hair was brown; it is now a beautiful grey. Later we realised we had a friend in common. She was the only candidate with a degree, which she gained as a mature student.

Scant regard was given to equal opportunities by members of the governing body, though to be fair, it was often done in ignorance of discrimination legislation. On another occasion, the shortlist for a bricklaying teacher was three men: two white and one black. Once all were interviewed, the chairman uttered without considering the merits of each interviewee, 'We'll appoint the blackie'. Perhaps fortunately for the appointment committee, the appointed candidate turned the job down. Subsequently the best candidate was appointed. In another case, I tried to help councillors decide on the best candidate to be offered the job. I began to say, 'Well, there are two weak candidates, two in the middle, and two strong candidates.' No sooner had I opened my mouth to offer advice when a councillor told me, sharply, that it was their decision on who was appointed and not mine.

There were instances where it was evident that a councillor had been lobbied on behalf of a candidate, or simply that the councillor wanted a particular candidate to be appointed for personal reasons. A small piece of paper would be shown to a few other councillors to ensure their candidate was appointed. I was lobbied a few times to put a candidate, known to a governor, on the short list. I was never approached to give the job to a candidate who was favoured by a councillor governor.

On another occasion a senior advisor in the authority applied to be Director of Education in the same authority. He failed to get the job. I was told sometime later by a member of the interview panel that he was not appointed because they assumed he was a member of Plaid Cymru because he spoke Welsh. It was later revealed that he was a member of the Labour Party and not Plaid Cymru.

I learned much about the power of a local education authority and the concomitant power of a college governing body, made up of politically elected Labour councillors. Sycophancy became the default behaviour by managers of some colleges in the relationship with members of political parties. Rhondda College had a close relationship with the House of Commons Speaker, George Thomas. On retirement he chose, as his ennobled title, Viscount Tonypandy. It is recorded in Leo Abse's *New Labour* that George Thomas included his new title 'Viscount' because of its incongruity with the Rhondda town of Tonypandy. Leo Abse wrote about George Thomas that: "Nowhere did he better illustrate his self-deprecation than in the title he assumed after retirement - Viscount Tonypandy. A casual observer might think this was homage to his birthplace in Wales. But there were politicos who understood his scoffing at the very viscountcy he was assuming. It was his way of coping with his tragic sense of his own unworthiness." Senior managers of Rhondda College fell for his joke and remained ignorant of George Thomas's wicked humour and went on to name their new restaurant - a converted classroom actually - The Viscount Tonypandy restaurant. George Thomas came along to open the restaurant.

Rhondda College had recently merged with Pontypridd College. On my first visit to do an initial assessment of facilities for students, a new library had been recently built with no access for disabled students to the first floor. The new library was given the name of the current chair of governors. In another part of the college, with no connection with the new library a toilet for disabled students had been created on the first floor, but there was no lift from the ground to first floor.

Ethical considerations seldom inhibited decisions made by governors consistent with their legal responsibilities, to which I alluded earlier. It is an absolute travesty more akin to a country characterised by unaccountable political leaders. Those engaged with such practices were referred to as members of the Taffia. An example of the wasteful practices of the Taffia was the decision not to relocate the headquarters of the newly created Mid-Glamorgan County in 1974, following local government reorganisation, but to leave the headquarters in the former County of Cardiff until 1996 when the County was abolished due to yet another local authority reorganisation. There are now 22 local authorities in Wales rather than the previous eight. Wales' politicians fell in love with Schumacher's theory that 'Small is Beautiful'! It was an open secret that councillors had decided that the headquarters remain in Cardiff so that their travelling expenses would be greater than if a new county hall had been located in the County of Mid-Glamorgan. At a meeting I attended an economist made an estimate of the retail revenue spent in Cardiff by officers, lunch time for example, by keeping Mid Glamorgan County Hall in Cardiff, at the expense of it being located in the boundary of Mid Glamorgan.

12: Tales of Brave Ulysses

To lead people, walk beside them. When the best leader's work is done, the people say, 'We did it ourselves!'

Lau Tsu

I have known every college principal in South Wales over three decades, through visiting their college while assessing students on teaching practice.

From the middle of the 1980s colleges became increasingly independent of local authorities. Successful progression to full independence is concomitant with an increase in the capacity of individual principals, and other senior managers, to cope with the new demands of managing an organisation. Nepotistic appointments now became few and far between, much less so than hitherto. During the early period of independence only two women were appointed Principals in South Wales. More were appointed over time, but they remained a significant minority.

Each Principal would manage in a manner that matched their leadership style, skills, values, competence, and size of college. Only one principal following the 1992 FHE Act had been a student in a further education college. The majority had humanities or history degrees. Not one had a serious management qualification.

Below I've headlined the personal characteristics of a few principals I knew well. Three of these were appointed through nepotism.

The cornet player

This Principal played the cornet in a brass band. Apparently, he was good at playing the cornet, but he was not a good principal. The college was the venue for a series of annual lectures in memory of a notable figure in the Labour party. The lectures attracted prominent public figures. On one occasion, the speaker was distinguished for her work in addressing poverty and hunger in Africa. It was an interesting and moving lecture. Press publicity had mentioned the lecture would be followed by an open buffet. However, this open invitation to the buffet was not communicated to those who were preparing the buffet; they had prepared a buffet for distinguished guests only. At the end of the meeting, the principal, in closing the evening, explained the buffet error and asked all present to join him in and experience what it is like to go short of food. It was whispered that he should have stayed playing the cornet. At a political husting, the Principal, when asked why he had not moved from Cardiff to the valley town, replied that the valley town was 'not for him, his wife or children.' On another occasion when he was addressing staff, soon after taking up post said, 'What this college needs is to GOYA - get off your arse'. This was never forgotten and confirmed in the minds of many that the distance between the valleys and Cardiff could be measured in more than miles.

His signature mannerism was to move his glasses quickly up and down in the manner of Eric Morecambe.

The engine fireman

The principal of a small valley college was appointed, having been the fireman of a train driver who was an extremely powerful local authority alderman. An alderman was a designated senior county councillor. In mitigation the fireman had completed a degree at Ruskin College, Oxford, as a mature student.

Has anyone seen management?

In reporting back to staff on the findings of a two-week inspection, the senior inspector remarked that, 'This college is a management free zone'.

He'll find a funeral ...

One Vice-Principal of a college which was under local education authority control was often not in his office. The story goes that he was due to receive a visitor. When the visitor arrived, the vice-principal could not be found. The visitor asked at reception where the vice-principal was. The receptionist answered, 'I'm sorry but he's gone to a funeral up the Rhondda.' The visitor, who lived in the Rhondda Fach, asked whose funeral it was. 'He wouldn't know', said the exasperated receptionist, 'But he's bound to find one.'

The word chiseller

This principal struggled to express himself, and he was fully aware of his shyness, and lack of social skills. It was said that he was appointed principal in return for the help his father gave to coal miners who needed to write their letters. It was strange that his writing skills were not learned by his son. He once said to me that he had to chisel every word onto letters, memorandum, and reports. On one occasion he invited a famous opera singer to speak at prize day. He was invited because he was born in a nearby village, and his mother still lived there. I introduced him to the opera singer and the opening sentence from the principal was, 'I've got all your records'. The latest government initiative became his latest jargon jumbled utterance. He thrived on the newest initiative to lubricate his tongue and speak incoherently to anyone he wished to impress. There was no serious attempt to internalise the initiatives so that visitors or colleagues might consider how they may be used to improve the college provision. He once said to me after one of his informal presentations to a visitor, 'Well, that went well'. On another occasion I was sitting in his room when he was talking on the phone to the local authority advisor for further education, Mr Jones, about the extra courses he wanted to introduce. Mr Jones would not agree with the principal's request, and in exasperation the principal forgot who he was speaking with, and uttered, 'It's that Jonesee who is putting the block on the new courses'. He subsequently uttered, 'I'm sorry Mr Jones'.

The narcissistic egotist

This principal had, seemingly, a high IQ but was also blessed with, undoubtedly, a marginally higher ego. His athletic larynx enabled him to think on his feet and get away with vacuous narcissistic remarks. He was not a modest man. He was lauded in the FE sector, but his reputation within the college was dismal. He created a think tank. A *think* tank it could never be. Internal to the college, it became known as a think *tub*. A *tub* was more fitting to a *tank's* capacity to generate creative ideas, with so many middle-management nepotistic management appointments. He would scan minutes of meetings of the board of governors, and not check them as an accurate record of the meeting. The minute clerk, who knew this, submitted the minutes for one meeting to be checked before being included in the governing body papers. The minute read '… at this point in the meeting the principal made a complete fool of himself.' The clerk was a kindly man and told the principal about the trick he had played on him. He was suspicious of the motives of many, especially me. I once overheard him saying on the phone to a local authority officer, 'You want to watch him'. He immediately realised that he ought not to have said that, not that he knew that I was overhearing him.

I'm from London

The Inner London Education Authority was formed in 1965 and dissolved in 1990. It was a highly politically left-wing local authority and attracted ridicule in the right-wing press. In today's language the authority had its fair share of wokes. The governor-dominated appointment board of the college was taken in by one female candidate's flourishing description of the London further education sector. She was appointed, and it wasn't long before she set about shaking the college out of its old ways. Her abrasive leadership style was not to the liking of the chair of governors, especially when she was appointed to the Wales NHS advisory board, an appointment he was expected to get. Her employment as Principal was short-lived.

The clever man

He was able, but seldom seen in the corridors of the college. I enjoyed a friendly and professional relationship with him. Lamentably, however, he would often be dismissive of female colleagues.

The boiler man

He would often be seen in the boiler room, wearing overalls. He was sacked due to budget failures.

As for me…

It seems counterintuitive, but I was fortunate to work with three weak leaders. Less than competent senior managers may allow those immediately below them the scope and freedom to do what they ought to be doing themselves, but for their failings.

As vice-principal I became suspicious of the quality of teaching of one particular English teacher. My suspicion arose when he wrote to me soon after I took up my post. I was not on my own with this suspicion when I learned that the team of English teachers would only timetable him on non-examination courses. I set about checking his qualifications. He had faked them. The qualifications were in the wrong order; the highest qualification was gained before the lower qualifications. The manager who gave him a reference for the English teacher post subsequently became the Principal of the college where he was found out. The story doesn't end there. Before I knew the teacher, he had been an English examiner for the WJEC. It all happened about thirty years ago.

A senior officer of the local authority of Mid Glamorgan asked if I would evaluate the professional development of FE teachers within the authority. Amongst other things it included an interview with the Director of Education and the Senior Advisor of schools. It was known that the Senior Advisor had *de facto* much more power and influence than the director, even though he was senior to the adviser. They had adjoining rooms in the corridor of the county hall. My first meeting was with the director. One question was: 'Do you think the authority school system will become tertiary in the future.' There was an emphatic 'Yes.' I moved next door to ask the senior adviser for schools with the same question. The response was an emphatic 'No.' The authority has only just gone tertiary in one of three authorities. It seems the junior officer had greater sway than the Director of Education. Such is the way in local authorities.

I became Wales' representative of the Association of Colleges, Beacon Awards. The CEO of the newly formed Association of Welsh Colleges asked if I would take over as the Wales representative. I accepted that principals in Wales had confidence that I would carry out the representative role with fairness and expertise. I continued in the position until retirement in 2007. The Beacon Awards were a means for colleges in further education to promote outstanding quality and innovative curriculum practices; the Awards were sponsored by companies engaged with colleges. On retirement, I became an assessor for the Awards. It involved visiting shortlisted colleges, then with a co-assessor agreeing on which one college should be nominated for a Beacon Award. The Awards were prestigious. Pontypridd college was outstandingly successful at being awarded Beacon prizes, and one year the college won three awards.

Shortly after retirement, I was accepted as a Reader (Assessor) for the Queen's Awards for Further and Higher Education. It continued for ten years, to this day. The parchment letter that confirmed that I would be a Reader emphasised that to be a Reader (Assessor) was an honour.

Each further education college is unique, and its range of courses reflects the industries and companies in the locality or region. Just as colleges are unique so, inevitably, are principals, as described above. Some are more modest than others.

There was one occasion where an immodest principal was caught out. Along with my co-assessor for a Beacon Award, I was welcomed to the college by the Principal and we were introduced to the person who had written the shortlisted Beacon submission. Assessment visitations and subsequent judgments become more reliable when a visit enables assessors to meet those deeply involved; teachers, managers, and students. On this visit the principal promoted himself, and took up an inordinate amount of time, leaving us insufficient time to speak to teachers. Consequently, it was impossible to form a judgement on their submission. By a remarkable coincidence, I was the assessor for the Queen's Award for Further and Higher Education for the same college and the same project. Both submissions failed

I was chairman of several Post-16 education organisations. The one I'm most proud of is the Valleys Initiative for Adult Education; this organisation became the lobby for the planned University of the Valleys. I was the first chairman of the Welsh for Adults organisation of South Wales. I chaired the Wales senior curriculum managers group; the Rhondda Cynon Taf, Family Learning Group, and the Welsh Government Community Consortium for Education and Training.

As chairman I would never dominate a committee. Typically, I would offer guidance and, where appropriate, ensure that all committee members were given the opportunity to contribute to the meeting, then summarise a provisional position which would usually lead to a resolution.

When chair, it would always be my intention to remain as chair for about four years; I would never divulge this was so, so as not to lose authority towards the end of my term of office. I took the view that about four years is an optimal period to chair an organisation. Currently I am Chair of Ysgol Gwaun y Nant (Welsh language primary school) Governing Board.

When I retired, senior officers of the Welsh government wrote acknowledging my significant contribution to Wales' further education.

13: A Wider Horizon

A ship in harbour is safe, but that is not what ships are for

John Augustus Shedd

While I was vice-principal there was a four-year period that coincided with the EU implementation of project funding to enable colleges from EU member states to meet, exchange ideas, and work together on vocational education projects. I became successful at writing curriculum development projects, and because of this, the college was invited to partner projects written and led by other colleges and universities in EU countries.

Colleagues were not paid extra for being away from home at weekends. The best the college could do was to cover all their out-of-pocket expenses, this was more often than not for drinks at the bar. I only had one rule for alcohol; I would say, 'I'll cover a few drinks, but not for becoming drunk.' It always worked. Early flights from Cardiff often required a taxi to the airport, with a typical journey being 30 miles. Two colleagues who were to meet me at the airport for a 06.30 flight to Amsterdam failed to meet the boarding gate on time. I fidgeted in my seat worrying about them, but just as the cabin door was due to close, they boarded the plane. The taxi had broken down 15 miles from the airport. They promptly paid the taxi driver for taking them halfway and called a friend at 05.30 to complete the journey. Now that's what I call kindness!

Success in securing a project was competitive, and as the EU programmes of projects became more widely known, competition increased. The medical condition I had, which was later diagnosed as cyclothymia, could at times be debilitating but it also gave me highs, and these highs contributed to my success in writing project proposals. They were always written at times away from college – at weekends or during closed periods. I say more about my cyclothymic condition in Chapter 15.

Once I had drafted the proposals, I would be mentally exhausted.

Writing bids for EU projects and visiting partners in continental Europe took up too much of my time as Vice-Principal. It was all getting too much for me. I needed assistance with administration, booking flights and hotels.

The senior manager of college administration tried to deny me a personal assistant (PA), even though I was bringing into the college six-figure project funds. Eventually, I found a way around this irrational behaviour by appointing a project assistant; all accounted for by project funds. What a coincidence that my project assistant allowed the title PA. All done and dusted. An additional benefit was that my new PA was very popular and a great source of inside information, if not gossip. I would be told of staff concerns or misdemeanours that I was unlikely to hear otherwise. This kind of information was a good touchstone and very helpful to me as a senior manager.

I was not unduly disappointed if a project submission failed. I was not excited if the submission was successful. It was the process of writing the project that stimulated both my intellect and my keen interest in EU vocational education.

The UK became a popular country to visit due, in part, to the English language. A consequence of this was that Pontypridd College had a large number of senior managers coming to visit. On one occasion there was a visitation from two senior managers from South-West Germany. When introducing themselves to the clerk of the college governing board they announced that they were from a vocational college in Baden-Baden. The clerk to the governing board introduced himself as living in the Rhondda valleys. The visitors, who had studied the locality of South Wales, asked the name of the village where the clerk of the governing body lived. He wickedly replied, 'Pentre-Pentre'. The visitors chuckled at the similarity of each other's area: Baden-Baden and Pentre-Pentre! No one dared say the Rhondda village was simply Pentre.

It was the same clerk to the college board of governors who would, when introducing the principal's report, refer to it as a *verbal* report, to the frustration of the board's chair, who would always correct him that it was an *oral* report and not a *verbal* report. The chair's frustration never

106

failed, and the clerk never learned.

An EU stipulation was that English would be the common language. This suited me, for sure. Yet being a first language English speaker was not without communication problems. Most European partners had learned English as a second language, and sometimes it was American business English. One social evening the conversation drifted into the limitations of speaking English as a second language. The Greek partner dryly remarked that the only person he had difficulty understanding was me, as a first language English speaker. His reasoning was that first language speakers will always have a nuanced vocabulary. Pidgin English was the shared language of project partners to aid communication. The idiosyncrasies of so-called Wenglish, the dialect of English spoken in the valleys, is illustrated in the following anecdote. A new county court was built in Merthyr and opened in the early years of the 1970s. It was located five minutes from the college. It provided an appropriate place to visit with students when the topic of the law was taught in Liberal Studies. One visit I arranged coincided with a grievous bodily harm case. I sat listening to the case with a class of students for about an hour. The defendant replied to a question put to him by the prosecuting barrister: 'You said that in your defence you had been drinking. How many pints had you had? The defendant answered, 'Only a couple'. The judge interjected sardonically, 'Is that a Welsh couple?' A couple in the valleys can be any single digit number!

I first began speaking to large groups while at University College, Cardiff. Speaking in European meetings in the EU compelled me to communicate clearly. Not unsurprisingly my Welsh accent was received as less pronounced, whether I was contributing to group discussion or in presenting a conference paper. A few moments before speaking at a conference I would be nervous, yet once I had completed the first few remarks I would always be relaxed, thus helping me to think and answer questions clearly. A humorous introductory remark would usually come to mind, putting me at ease and hopefully conference members. I would aim to find a rhythm to my presentation, thus facilitating a confident analysis and communicating associations within the subject.

Notwithstanding how much I enjoyed speaking on a subject about which I was confident, I can remember almost 'freezing' on one occasion, and it was in my college. I was about to introduce a conference on a new prospectus developed by all training organisations in the locality. There I stood behind the lectern, when suddenly my mind went blank. I recovered instantly, but it was a most unsettling experience.

The most significant two conferences I talked at were international, and each had the prefix 'The first world conference...'. One was in Munich with the title 'The first world congress for the motor industry'. The other was at the University of Pendidikan, Indonesia, and was entitled 'The first world congress for technical and vocational education and training'.

European conferences became much more accessible to FE staff than was previously the case, thanks to EU funding. Prior to the expansion of funding to promote European vocational and training programmes, including curriculum development and student exchanges, overseas visits and conferences were largely the domain of HE. With European project partners we won a United Nations award for developing a curriculum on recycling products with Bremen University.

In addition to European curriculum projects, there were study tours. I was successful at getting a place on every one that I applied for. I had developed a knack of writing applications. I was a frequent visitor to EU universities, the purpose for these visits being to share ideas on training programmes and consider the design of curricula. I became a frequent speaker at EU conferences on innovative curriculum models developed at Pontypridd College. I went to Seattle in the USA and several colleges in South Africa. My visit to Seattle was arranged by an organisation to foster EU/USA vocational education links. The visit to South Africa was to Johannesburg, Pretoria, and Soweto townships, organised by the British Council. The poverty and living conditions in the townships were awful. We were welcomed into the townships for it was an opportunity for those living there to receive voluntary payment for allowing their photographs to be taken of them.

The purpose of the British Council project was to meet middle managers of technical colleges to brief them on their three month visit to UK colleges to shadow senior managers. The FE colleges built for white students were similar to UK FE colleges, but with a disturbing sign at the entrance stating 'No guns'. The colleges for black students were poorly resourced. However, these colleges were far more creative in the way limited resources were used. The visiting college managers from Johannesburg were shocked that UK students would be late for classes, and many would not attend regularly. The visiting manager that I tutored had social and cultural attitudes akin to the Victorian era.

I read up on the political and social conditions of South Africa in preparation for the visit. Although I was thus well prepared, my anxiety increased on arrival, since there were so many gated houses with guards and dogs, and the daunting 'No guns' signs. On one occasion I nervously went to a nearby supermarket. I was so anxious I could not get back to the hotel quickly enough.

Because I travelled overseas frequently, I had my fair share of duty-free cigars and whisky. I bought and drank too much whisky. I started smoking cigars. They were Villager cigars. At first, buying *The Guardian* newspaper promoted a left-wing political persona, now buying Villager cigars reinforced that left-wing persona. I have never smoked cigarettes, and Villager cigars didn't last long, along with my desperate attempt to be raffish.

There was an occasion when, with two colleagues, I had a two-day meeting in Paris. We had been warned of the prevalence of pickpockets. Being a little nervous about this, I put most of my francs, the pre-Euro French currency, into my shoes for safekeeping. We walked a great deal, taking advantage of our free time to do a bit of sightseeing. On returning to my hotel bedroom, I took my shoes off. To my horror, the franc notes had worn away, aided by sweaty feet.

Another time two colleagues and I had a visit to Trentino in Italy. We stayed overnight in Milan before catching the train in the early morning. That evening we went to the railway station to get our tickets for the morning train. One colleague had been taking an evening Italian language course at our college for four years. He was a very proud man, and a bit prickly. But here was his chance to ask for the three tickets in Italian. He had barely finished his first sentence when the ticket officer said, 'Do you mind speaking English?' So much for the four years learning Italian.

Another humorous story was when one of my colleagues pointed out something about the aircraft we had flown in from Cardiff to Amsterdam to our hosts. With Amsterdam being the headquarters of KLM, Pontypridd College wanted to explore the possibility of exchanging staff and students in aircraft maintenance. It seemed a good match with Pontypridd College training apprentices for General Electric (formally BA) aircraft engine maintenance and the Amsterdam college doing similar work for KLM. The aircraft we flew over on was a small Fokker, widely used by KLM on their 'City Hopper' services. During our tour of the college's workshops, my colleague noticed a poster of the Fokker we had flown over on. He remarked with some interest that it was 'the little Fokker we flew over in'.

Of all the project visits and European conferences, one of the funniest moments was during a conference in Italy. There was a discussion about incompetent teachers and the way respective countries manage the problem. The Netherlands representative said that once all support measures had been exhausted and improvement remains unacceptable, we *fire* the teachers. The translation came back as 'In the Netherlands, we *shoot* them'.

There was one EU programme designed to facilitate UK colleges liaison with East German colleges. I needed to take a colleague who spoke German to translate during meetings. On this occasion, we visited two colleges in Leipzig. One college principal invited us to his home to meet his family over dinner. There was much to discuss about our respective technical education systems, and much alcohol was consumed throughout the evening. It got to the point where my colleague, who was with me to translate, enjoyed himself so much that he stopped translating. It was a little later, with a chuckle in my voice, that I diplomatically reminded him why I had brought him with me – to act as my translator. Back at our hotel on the way home, we took a sauna. To our surprise, if not delight, two women joined us and casually became topless. We got even warmer. Of course, we learned later that this is the custom.

I became involved with the Declaration of Human Rights through an EU curriculum development project. The project results were published in a handbook for technical teachers at vocational schools across the EU. I played a major role in developing curricular models to promote human rights across subjects and vocational areas. Of note is one curriculum model called the 'Shadow Curriculum'. The introduction to the handbook states: 'One of the most important chapters is on the 'Shadow Curriculum'. The model is a concept for providing teachers with a pool of information and methodology for linking technology with human rights issues.

In addition to visiting continental Europe, I went to Oman to advise on vocational courses for the prestigious World Bank. I got into deep trouble while going to Oman. The invitation to accept the request to go to Oman was too irresistible though I knew that my cautious principal would not wish me to go. Indeed, while I was in Oman, he copied me into an email to the head of construction praising him for concentrating on local objectives. I was distressed by this email because I knew it was written to disturb me. On return a while later, my principal phoned me, and I worried that the summons might herald the possibility that I might be dismissed for going to Oman. It was later that the principal told me that he was frightened to tell me about the whole story and what was behind it. It was no secret that the college finance officer and I had different views of college management. The finance officer saw his chance to get me sacked. He assumed that I had gone to Oman while continuing to receive my salary. That I would never do. He did in effect blow the whistle on me. I had prior, to leaving for Oman, written to the principal explaining that my salary would be covered by the World Bank.

An investigation followed by the college internal auditors. Not only was I exonerated by members of the college audit committee, but I was praised for accepting the invitation from the World Bank. When it became known that it was the college finance officer who was the whistle-blower, it was realised he had come within a moment of being summarily sacked by the college chair of governors.

Pontypridd College hosted a group of students from the UAE. The group of fifteen students were at our college for six months to learn English, before moving on to train as firefighters at a college in the West of England. The College didn't have its own student accommodation, so it was arranged for the students to live with local families. We had two students in our home. On the first Sunday, I gave them a walking tour of Merthyr. When passing a pub, I said, 'But of course your culture will not allow you to drink alcohol'. To which they responded, 'Yes, but it's important that we learn your ways!' The students were immediately uninhibited when meeting the college's hairdressing students; with a few falling in lust. But lusting and learning English came all too soon for some. The time came for the students to move on to the firefighting college. As they got on the coach, they waved goodbye with, 'Tara'. So much for their English language course. It was a short while later that the owner of the nearest newsagent remarked to a colleague that the sale of *Playboy* magazine reduced immediately on the group's departure.

The UK government instructed further education colleges from 1992 onwards to work more directly with employers. For me, this provided a wonderful opportunity to encourage colleagues to contact companies to see how the college might meet their skills needs. This objective was timely, as the UK was entering the EU single market in 1993.

Many contacts were made with employers leading to commercial courses designed for individual companies. As a means of informing employing organisations about the EU Single Market, I created, and subsequently chaired, Mid-Glam Euro Club. It proved to be a highly successful club for employers and the college's subsequent involvement in EU projects. It was through Euro Club that I made my first EU visit to Majorca, organised by the European Forum for Vocational Education and Training (EFVET). There I met people who would later become partners in EU funded vocational curriculum projects. Much later, I became chair of the UK branch of EFVET. Besides promoting EFVET in the UK, it required occasional weekend meetings in Brussels. Mostly I would fly from Bristol, but on two occasions I went by Eurostar and paid the extra to be in business class; this I enjoyed greatly.

Euro Club was an exemplary innovation of college engagement with local companies. Lamentably, however, it did not have the support of a couple of senior managers. It is well researched that innovators are not necessarily well received by all, and this is the case with me. In fact, my Bachelor degree dissertation studied innovation. I was fully committed to the purpose of Euro Club and could see the benefits to local employers and the college.

For one Euro Club meeting we invited chargés d'affaires from several European countries. It attracted many local employers. The main speaker was a professor from the motor industry faculty of Bremen University. There followed a plenary session with the chargés d'affaires on the panel. Questions and answers followed in the usual way, concentrating on respective countries. One attendee asked more than his fair of questions. When he asked a question of the French chargé d'affaire, he spoke in an accent of a French person speaking English. When he asked a question of the German University of Bremen professor, he spoke in the guttural accent of the German language. It went on in a similar manner with a couple of more questions to other chargés d'affaires. By this time, there was muffled laughter from attendees. I chaired the conference and had to keep a serious face. I just about did it, thank goodness. I thanked the chargés d'affaire for their presence and attendees for coming. I did it in a Welsh accent!

A couple of employees of a Welsh Government quango, with a remit to assist Euro Club, failed to do so. Notwithstanding the quango's lamentable lack of support, the club ran for many years and attracted great praise from local companies.

FE colleges in Wales have a low turnover of teachers; this has advantages and drawbacks. One drawback is that teachers may not be exposed to new teaching methodologies. Visits to EU colleges provided opportunities for teachers to share teaching experiences and forms of vocational curriculum and quality systems across several member states of the European Union.

Further, initial meetings with project partners would involve describing our respective colleges, curriculum, quality systems and related practices. Describing Pontypridd College many times to our EU partner colleges became a rehearsal for our merger talks with staff in two local colleges that subsequently merged with Pontypridd College.

14: Village, Town, City, Country

His nerves of metal and his blood oil ...(he) runs his engine on different fuel

R. S. Thomas *Cynddylan on a Tractor*

My place of birth was my mother's sister's house, opposite my parents' home, where my mother still lives in Aberfan.

My first move was to London in 1967, where I lived in digs near Wembley while working for Rolls Royce. There I stayed for four years before returning to Merthyr for marriage. For a short while, we lived with my sister-in-law and husband. It was not a happy state, but where else were we to live while waiting for mortgage approval? Getting a mortgage in those days was not the simple online procedure as it is today. It involved an interview with the mortgage society branch manager. In the intervening period we lived in a council flat at the foot of the Brecon Beacons, in a former sanatorium. There we lived with our first child. I have to admit I took a while to settle down to parenthood. I kept up my friendship with a group I had known for a long time; always meeting in a pub.

From there, we moved to a seventies style housing estate in the hillside village of Heolgerrig, overlooking the town of Merthyr. There were two pubs, a general store and a primary school, where our daughter went. [Overheard two children from Heolgerrig – pronounced ilgerrig by many: 'Why is ilgerrig called ilgerrig? 'Because it's on *an* il'.] At least the preposition 'an' for 'il' is correct.

The corruption of the word Heolgerrig to ilgerrig is an example of nouns heard in Welsh Government *Designated Dialect Preservation Zones* – my term!

This was a period where there were frequent dinner parties, where we and our friends were proud to show our new family homes. Even though my first career in the motor industry involved much manual work, I was not a natural manual worker. On one occasion we wished to impress our friends with our new IKEA paintings. Not having sufficient time to secure them to the wall with permanent fittings, I

115

stuck them to the wall with BluTack. Inevitably, the dining room during the evening got warmer. It reached a temperature where the BluTack let me down and one by one the IKEA painting slipped down the dining room walls ingloriously, seemingly between each course!

We were extremely happy here with our young family and friends, many of whom were struggling with the financial and emotional demands of young families. It was the time where I was devoting every spare minute to studying for my degree; I was determined to get a First. I would spend long periods learning to write quickly and form precise sentences, without correction. I planned how I would present paragraphs on the examination papers. I felt that our future took on an inordinate importance, due to my determination to improve my career prospects.

We moved from the seventies housing estate to an area of the town where people had professional occupations or their own businesses. There we stayed for fifteen years until we divorced. This parting was not acrimonious, however, and we still have concern for each other. Divorce was my opportunity to go south to the Cardiff area. It was a move I had longed for, but not the circumstances. My mother tried her hardest to get me to live in her sister's house, in the same street, that had recently been put up for sale. Any doubt that I had been brought up in an enmeshed family vanished instantly.

Following a short while in Dynas Powys, near Cardiff, we bought a new house in Pencoedtre, Barry, which was on the first phase of a large new housing development. The Lidl store is the centrepiece of the barren estate. Had it not been for the attraction of Lidl we would not have bought the house! We called into Lidl for a loaf of sliced bread, and there we remembered our daughter mentioning the new houses that were just being built. We called into the show house, where we were shown a house that was almost completed and had been reduced by £15,000 due to the original buyers dropping out. When we moved into our new home a neighbour asked if we were the couple who bought the house while buying a sliced loaf!

The nationwide house builder referred us to their preferred solicitor to expiate the contract and arrange for our Dynas Powys home to be bought by the building firm and used as part-exchange for the Pencoedtre house. While signing the contract in the solicitor's office, confirming the address of the house, I said it was in Barry, to which he advised that the address should be Pencoedtre and not Barry. Much later I would refer to Pencoedtre as West Wenvoe; Wenvoe is posh! Shopping in Lidl a few years later I overheard someone remark on the snobbery of calling the location of the Pencoedtre estate, West Wenvoe. Lidl and Barry have been a great source of humour for my wife and me; we refer to it variously as the German delicatessen, and the Harrods of Barry.

Our mortgage interest rate and the amount we borrowed was just about what we could afford due to our age. At the time credit card companies were offering interest free deals and we managed our finances through taking out several credit card loans. We moved seven years later and now live in the country village of Wenvoe, seven miles west of Cardiff. The contract purchase deal, with a different house builder, was again part-exchange.

15: Salad Days

The greatest wealth is health

Virgil

When I retired, depression and anxiety hit me as a mental illness, like never before. Though I had lived with mild mental illness for several decades. It was adrenalin that had hid it from colleagues while I worked as a vice-principal for twenty years. My GP, whom I had been seeing for depression for around ten years, and who had prescribed antidepressants and would sometimes block double sessions to allow me to talk through my condition, eventually referred me to a clinical psychologist. I had twenty-two sessions of cognitive analytical therapy. The weekly sessions helped me to understand the consequences of being the black sheep of an enmeshed family, something I always knew, as I explain in Chapter 1. It was she who wrote in a letter after reading this book that: 'The world needs restless souls like you to challenge and organise the rest of us to move things forward.' An adaptation of this sentiment is the statement on the top of the front cover.

The clinical psychologist helped me to move on. She suggested that it might help me to draw the source of my mental pain. This I did on a small rectangular card for the next session with her. There are two colours, black at the top of the card and light blue at the bottom. The texture of the black is rough, representing coal mining and the dominant socio-economic culture of the South Wales valleys. The blue is smooth, representing the socio-economic culture of Cardiff and the sea, where I was living, in the Vale of Glamorgan. The card is in our bedroom. Its impact on me remains remarkably therapeutic, and it serves as a visual narrative of fundamental decisions and emotions in my life. At one of our sessions, the psychologist asked if I would wish to be without my psychological struggles. I said no. I was getting better at managing the condition. Stoicism and early failure give me curiosity, creativity, and determination that I would not want to lose. On completing the programme, she gifted me a book, 'Jonathan Livingston

Seagull (Richard Bach). It's on a bookshelf.

Later, I was referred to a psychiatrist for medical assessment by my GP. I was given a letter that my GP had written to the psychiatrist. This letter mentioned that I had lived through the Aberfan disaster and that I was an intelligent man. After a couple of years of assessments by the psychiatrist, my condition was diagnosed as cyclothymia. It is a milder form of bipolar disorder and is characterised by cyclical mood swings. However, the highs and lows are not severe enough to qualify as either mania or clinical depression.

Profoundly relevant to explaining my cyclothymia condition was the stark change in my upbringing in a valley town to living in a village near Cardiff. The gulf in the socio-cultural environment of the two is dramatic.

Valley towns have never fully recovered from the rapid closure of the coal mines in the1980s. In contrast, Cardiff, the capital of Wales, has thriving retail and finance sectors and a rich provision of culture, together with the Welsh Parliament in the Senedd.

For a long period after my retirement, my wife and I would not take a holiday, due to the unpredictability of my moods. With medication, my mental illness is much improved, and I've learned to live with it, with the strong support of my wife, who before retirement was a university teacher of psychology. Thank goodness, I have enjoyed good physical health and still do, even now at seventy-eight. Medication has help me to live with cyclothymia. The condition came to an abrupt crisis when I was shopping in a large retail store. Blackness hit me; I had to put my head on a clothes rail. It was awful, like no other condition. I questioned myself as to the point of my existence. This episode lasted a few minutes. It was ten years later that I spoke about it to my wife, when she came with me to review my medication with the psychiatrist. The cocktail list of medication prescribed is Lamotrigine, Mirtazapine, Fluoxetine and Diazepam. A short while ago, I had a brain scan. The consultant reported that I had a pristine brain, and he only hoped that his brain would be in my condition when he got to my age.

Living with cyclothymia was not helped when for several years I

119

subscribed to too many weekly political magazines: *The Spectator, The Economist, New Statesman* and *Prospect.* Added to this I took three Sunday papers: *The Sunday Times, The Observer* and at the weekend *The Financial Times.* This caused me great anxiety in being desperately keen to be informed of current affairs. My reading is now reduced to online editions of *The Times, The Guardian,* and *The Spectator.* Though I am much more relaxed with just having three publications, I'm plagued to this day with ruminating.

Further, drinking much too much over a long period did not help my cyclothymia. I started drinking alcohol when I was about twenty-one, which is quite old by today's standards. From then on until I was seventy, I would drink quite freely, even though it was at the expense of my mental health, and I suppose physical health. In my first marriage, we would sit together of an evening, and I would frequently drink several glasses of whisky. I stopped drinking whisky when I remarried, instead turning to wine. I might drink a bottle a night. Then six years ago I suddenly stopped drinking. I have been abstemious ever since. My life has changed. No hangovers anymore, even mild ones. One consequence of drinking too much was the onset of Type 2 diabetes. This is now managed with a healthy lifestyle.

I was a workaholic throughout my career in education, which is no good to anyone, especially those closest to you. Yet I was not driven at all when working in the motor industry. My primary drive then was to move away from a valley village. My aim in education was to get a first-class degree and become a senior manager in a further education college. Now that I am retired, I am close to living in the present.

When I am on a cyclothymia high there are times when I spend too much. I continue to buy clothes, and clothes towards the top end of the price range. There are few times that I will pay full price for an item, but I don't try hard enough *not* to buy an item if it is reduced. I'm more likely to buy clothes and cars when I'm on a high. When I look at excess clothes in my wardrobes, I'm looking at my medicine cabinets.

For several years at Pontypridd College, I would wear a fresh flower in my lapel each morning. Also, in an extended period of a high mood, I tended to overdo air-kissing female colleagues who were friends. I

120

have always been tactile, but during this high phase, I probably went over the top. Air-kissing is not the usual form of kissing in the South Wales valleys and its novelty is, probably, how I got away with it. When we were members of the EU, air-kissing failed to cross the English Channel and consequently wind its way up the valleys. Now that the UK has left the EU, there is *no* chance that air-kissing will try again and find its way to Pontypridd. After all, air-kissing in continental fashion has only just reached Cardiff, outside of the professional classes.

Old age has purloined my flamboyance, and now I'm likely to buy *quiet* clothes that do not bring attention to myself. Sad to say the young peacock has morphed into the dying swan! Blue framed spectacles are my one concession to earlier flamboyance.

Recently I undertook an *audit* of my clothes. I have far too many of everything. I counted them all and put each item in descending order of number: shirts 85, summer socks 75, summer jumpers 75, T-shirts 60, shoes 40, underpants 35, trousers 34, winter hats 30, summer hats 26, winter jumpers 22, jackets 22, summer scarves 19, winter scarves 17, Polo shirts 15, jeans 13, snoods 13, shorts 11, handkerchiefs 10, bandanas 10, leather belts 8, Barbour style jackets 5, suits 4, winter and summer jackets 19, rain jackets 3, swimming shorts 3, trainers 1, gilet 1. Amongst the 19 jackets is one I paid 5,000 Australian Dollars for. I was on a cyclothymic high with jet lag and taken in by the smart talking shop owner. It's a lovely jacket, though!

Of the 60 T-shirts, ten are Breton striped T-shirts. I bought the Breton T-shirts over a single month, taking my current bank account into the red. I became obsessed with getting all Breton T-shirts on-line and in shops. They had to be genuine Breton T-shirts, which have twenty-one navy blue stripes. In my sartorial medicine cabinet Breton T-shirts represent my *overdose* along with the *lovely* jacket.[*lovely*, is one of those words we *love* in Wales!]

Cars have played a decreasing interest in my life. As an apprentice motor mechanic, it was unsurprising that I enjoyed cars when young. My parents bought my first car, an Austin A40. For a short period, I also had an MG TD. Rushing to prepare this MG for the road might well have taken my life on its first road test because I had failed to repair the steering system properly. This example of rushing to have a test run illustrates my tendency, on occasion, to be rather slipshod. Another example, outside of motor cars, is when we bought our first house. It had a coal fire, with the grid removed by the previous owner. I replaced the grid from a scrap yard. It was not a perfect fit, so I filled in the gaps with industrial adhesive, rather than a special cement for a fireplace grid. It was commonplace at the time to bank the fire, which is to say add small lumps of coal before going to bed so that the fire would remain burning slowly all night. On the first morning we entered the living room to find the grid adhesive had melted and a number of coals had spilled out onto the hearth, dangerously close to the carpet.

After the MG I bought a new Mini. The Mini was the car of the moment; it was owned by celebrities. It had a transverse engine and gearbox in one. It was an engineering breakthrough; the novel power unit allowed for a small car to have the passenger area of a much larger traditional car. It seated four; though there would be newspaper photographs showing the car cramped with as many people as possible; thirteen I remember being the most. There followed upgraded variations. I had a new Riley Elf. Riley was a high-quality British carmaker. There was a Hornet, a version of the Mini by another British motor manufacturer, Wolseley. There was a Mini Cooper. The Cooper car maker was known for its success in producing racing cars. The Mini car and its derivatives are now owned by BMW, another case which illustrates the decline of British car manufacturing.

When in London, I had a new MG midget. Can you imagine a car called a midget today? If 'midget' is inputted to a computer, it converts to dwarf! A royal blue convertible. It was this car that I did a 180-degree spin when dashing back to London early one Monday morning. I had driven just three miles when I spun around on black ice. I was now facing my way home. What should I do, go back home, or carry on to London? I turned around and arrived at Rolls Royce in time for work. I felt quite proud of myself that my decision was to press on to London.

A new MG midget was about the same price in 1966 as a Morgan. The Morgan car is built in Malvern and is still considered an attractive purchase. MG cars could be purchased by walking into a car showroom. In contrast, there was a waiting list of about six months for a Morgan. The Morgan is a much better car, is coach-built and timeless. The essential style is the same today as in 1966. This is another case of my compulsion to buy immediately. So much for deferred gratification – an assumed behaviour of the middle-class, I was desperate to be. I had two Renaults; both died on me. Two cars caught fire due to my fault caused by my slipshod work, again. Yet being slipshod is the last thing I was when working in education. The first caught fire from a car radio I had fitted. Car radios were not integral with the car as they are today. They were bolt-on accessories. In my case, I had fitted it and done something wrong with the cables. The second car caught fire when we were taking our daughter to ballet lessons. She gave ballet up after that; she seemed not to be disappointed.

Then I went upmarket and bought a used Saab, with heated front seats and an empty tank of petrol. It just loved petrol, and I hated her for it. That was another car that died on me. By this time, I was vice-principal at Pontypridd College with my own parking space, though incidentally I never really enjoyed this privilege. From there I went down market with another Renault, but at least it was better on petrol. Then up market again to another Saab. A new Citroen car followed while I was still at Pontypridd College. I kept this for nine years, which was too long. It died of old age.

Then on retirement, I went on a spending spree. I bought a used black E-class Merc, which I kept for two years. Then a used silver-grey C-class Merc, which I kept for one year. There followed a gunmetal E-class Merc for two years. Then a white E-class Merc, followed by a new white C-class Merc. I've now got a red A-class Merc that I have had for four years. It may be my last car.

In listing all my cars, it is only now, in writing my memoir, that I see that buying so many Mercs over a short number of years is a symptom of the same cyclothymia which afflicted my habit of frequently buying new clothes. Still, it is almost over with cars, but not quite over with clothes.

16: The Welsh Language

I am Welsh by birth, English by education and European by nature

Peter Greenaway

My father learned English at six years of age when he began school. Until that time, he spoke only Welsh. My mother only spoke English. She would be irritated when my father spoke to his relations in Welsh. The Welsh language ended in the family with my father not using the language with my sister and me. It was not unusual at the time for Welsh not to be spoken to children where only one parent spoke Welsh, and this is still the case in many families.

Since retirement, I have joined several Welsh learners' classes, and I'm still doing so. However, I can't *fully* open the gate to Welsh culture without greater fluency in the language. Even so I enjoy attending Welsh language social and cultural events and learning more about Welsh traditions with my wife, who speaks Welsh as her first language. It has taken me into a Wales *new* to me, that has enriched my life much more than when I was an *80-minute nationalist* during international rugby games. I have been converted to the campaign to put a penis on the flag's dragon as it is on the £1 coin and an even bigger one on the £2 coin - it's true! My only reservation in supporting the flag penis campaign is its wobbling on a windy day.

Getting older has made my sense of *loss* of the Welsh language a continuing frustration. Though how can you *lose* something you never had? I wish so much that my father had spoken to me in Welsh at an early age. I find it problematic not to speak Welsh with almost all my education career spent in Wales. It's reasonable to say that I would have had more senior positions in the education sector had I been a Welsh speaker.

The decline of the Welsh language has been arrested due to the determination of senior Welsh speaking officers in the education sector since the 1950s. A debt is owed to the vision and drive of those in influential positions who argued for establishing Welsh-medium primary schools and later secondary schools. The growth of Welsh-medium schools has been remarkable, with over twenty per cent of pupils in Welsh-medium primary schools. The development will continue to increase, with the Welsh government setting a target of fifty per cent of the Welsh population to speak Welsh by 2050.

Both our children went to English medium schools. The nearest, Welsh-medium secondary school was fifteen miles away in another county. At the time, my wife and I shared a view that our children should attend a local *community* school. A generation later, I influenced my daughter to send her children to a Welsh-medium primary school and then to a Welsh-medium secondary school, even though the secondary school was in another valley. By this time, I had increased my understanding of Welsh culture and the use of the Welsh language in employment. It's interesting to see how our two families of grandchildren view the Welsh language. One family of grandchildren love the Welsh language and its culture; they use Welsh out of school and are fortunate that their grandmother, a first language Welsh speaker, lives locally. In contrast, our other grandchildren live too far away to have the advantage of speaking Welsh frequently with their grandmother. Their use of Welsh is broadly confined to school. I've noticed that our two grandchildren in Australia, who spent their early years in Wales and went to a Welsh reception school, now in their teens, seem to have quite soft Australian accents.

The National Eisteddfod of Wales was held in Cardiff in 2018. I was on a Welsh learners' course (again!) that year. With the Eisteddfod being in Cardiff, the director of the Welsh Learners' Centre asked our class if nine of us would be interested in forming a choral group to sing at the Eisteddfod. I put my name forward, and the nine of us started practising two months before the week of the Eisteddfod. A group of nine singers was the Eisteddfod stipulation and all in the group should be learning Welsh. Our course tutor led our practice sessions, with notes being indicated with the position of his guitar. High notes would be indicated by the guitar pointing upwards, whilst for low notes the guitar would be pointed downwards. Moderate notes were indicated with the guitar being somewhere in the middle. We practised four popular Welsh songs. There were four groups of nine when we arrived at the hall for the competition.

The first group of women were uniformly dressed as Michael Jackson (traditional Welsh consume!). The second group wore evening dresses, well suited for an evening performance at the Welsh National Opera. The third group and our group wore casual clothes. The first two groups sang in harmony. The third was an acapella group, who also sang in harmony. Then it was our turn. We sang with gusto, ensuring we followed the movement of the leader's guitar. The emotion was absolutely exhilarating. The panel of judges announced their decision. We came third!

Just one comment on this chapter: My English monoglot maternal grandmother attended a Welsh Baptist chapel for years, to be with her Welsh-speaking friend, despite not understanding a word of Welsh, not even the hymns.

17: Retirement

Old teachers never die: they just grade away

Anonymous

I retired in October 2007 after two careers spanning thirty-seven years: twelve years in the motor vehicle industry and twenty-seven in further and higher education. My wife retired a year later. We continue to maintain our interest in all sectors of education and we both take great interest in current affairs. Most of our news comes from the radio and online newspapers and magazines. My reading is limited to political biographies and current political books, while my wife's reading is eclectic. She also reads much more than me.

I had a good pension, with a lump sum payment, on retirement. It enabled us to move from Barry to Wenvoe. Apart from an earlier mortgage we have been rather injudicious with our finances. We share our finances completely and discuss buying exceptional items together. We looked forward to travelling in retirement, but apart from holidays abroad when recently retired, we now enjoy being home, with a few holidays in hotels that take dogs.

Through work, especially when vice-principal, many colleagues became friends. Time passes. I've been retired for sixteen years, and I see several former colleagues for coffee occasionally, with the meetings becoming less frequent.

I continued with a few consultancies with one friend for a couple of years. One of our contracts was to write a college submission for a Beacon Award, a prestigious award in further education. A good submission is only good if the subject of the submission is worthy of an award. In this case, undoubtedly, the excellent subject was helped by our writing of the submission; it became the President's Beacon Award in 2013. The President's Prize is presented to the college with the most innovative curriculum project in the UK.

On moving to Wenvoe, in the Vale of Glamorgan, we took up volunteering. My wife volunteers in the village library and is active in matters concerning the Welsh language. I have kept my work as a Reader for the Queen's Award. I'm chair of governors at a local Welsh language primary school, and a governor of a further education college. For a while, I wrote the front page for the village magazine.

We wake early, at about five, then listen to Radio 4 and Times Radio until our morning walk with our dog Mali, then I go to the gym for an hour or so, several days a week. On return from walking Mali, we do our own thing, meeting up later and certainly for dinner. We separate again until bedtime, with Radio 4 or Times Radio on in the background. We will often leave the radio on all night, with the World Service drifting in and out of our sleep. We listen to the radio much more than watching television.

Perhaps it takes retirement to make new friends; this is so with us. Our neighbours and new friends are well educated, with former careers in the professions. It is such a delight to share our retirement with those who provide stimulation with plenty of good humour, and without the need to impress. We share some friendship groups, village social and development meetings. I put myself forward as a candidate for a community councillor. I came in as the best of the losers. Nothing was lost, however: I got to know Wenvoe village by putting my canvassing leaflet in every house.

Within weeks of retirement, I wanted to see if I could cope with jobs without the sort of backup that had been available to me when I was a college vice-principal. This I did by becoming a Mystery Shopper. For instance, in a college there are those you can draw on if your computer fails; those that will solve a failed printer; those that will produce PowerPoint programmes; those who will proofread your papers; colleagues to help advise on policy, and so on.

I had assignments for banks, mobile telephones shops, a government benefits office, and a few hotels and pubs. I was nervous on my early assignments and felt like a faux customer, which I was. Preparation prior to a visit was remembering a lengthy checklist of what to look for or questions to ask of those working in a bank or shop, for instance. Once the mystery visit was over, I would return home to input the completed checklist. I think I was rumbled on three assignments: a bank, a government benefits office, and while having a hotel breakfast. At the government benefits office I had to inquire, on behalf of a family member, about the qualifying criteria for claiming benefits when unable to work due to anxiety. I could see on the face of the person behind the desk that I was doing no such thing as inquiring on behalf of a family member. All assignments had one observation in common, which was waiting time before being seen by an assistant. The pay was £10 per assignment and £50 for one bank assignment, which needed to be completed that day. Each bank had two observations amongst others; one was to note if there was litter directly outside of the bank and if the latest promotion posters were displayed inside.

I soon got fed up with being a mystery shopper and finished after two months. Well, at least I did get close to achieving my reason for doing it, which was to see if I could cope with jobs on my own. I think I did it.

I met a BBC Wales retired investigative journalist in a Cardiff coffee shop by chance. He was sitting with a friend, and I recognised him and his distinctive voice. A couple of weeks earlier, he had written an interesting piece on education for the Institute of Welsh Affairs (IWA). In passing, I stopped to say how much I enjoyed reading the article and how it had mentioned several people known to me from my time in further and higher education. He thanked me and asked if I had heard of *Wales Eye*. No, was the answer.

Soon afterwards, having read a few pieces of *Wales Eye*, I plucked up the courage to send him the first satirical piece I had ever written. To my surprise, it appeared in *Wales Eye* within days; it was the Autumn of 2014. A once-weekly satirical piece followed; it became two pieces a week within a few weeks. This continued for two stimulating years. To my surprise, I could write political satire! Almost all my items were about life in the Welsh Assembly. I stopped writing for *Wales Eye*, rather abruptly. However, the same day the editor of *Wales Politico*, a daily blog, phoned to ask if I would write for his blog. *Wales Politico* was a more serious blog than *Wales Eye*, and I was pleasantly surprised to be invited to write political satire for a respected political blog. Within a week or so to my amazement a few of my Wales Politico pieces began appearing in *'The Wales Yearbook - best of the day's blogs'*. It continued for a couple of months until *Wales Politico* closed. A few years later I compiled for publication a selection of pieces from *Wales Eye* and *Wales Politico* with the title 'There is life in the Senedd' - the home of the Welsh Parliament. Before that book, I co-authored a book of humorous stories from my career in education. The book had the title 'Chalkface Chuckles'. Both are for sale on Amazon.

The IWA is the leading think tank in Wales. I went through a period of writing for the IWA on subjects I considered worthy of public debate. Issues included: the EU Brexit referendum, protecting public space, further education, Welsh government and more. One of my pieces was on notable persons of Wales. The person I wrote about was the world-renowned architect, Zaha Hadid, who was commissioned to design the Wales opera house in Cardiff Bay, funded by the UK Millennium development project. Such projects throughout the UK were selected for their purpose and architecture.

The opera house was never built, with one reason being given (unofficially) that it was called an *opera* house with its connotation of high culture. High culture in Wales does not garner votes for politicians. At a later date the UK Millennium Commission supported a development project to the reconfiguring of the national rugby stadium Cardiff Arms Park, in time for Wales hosting the 1999 Rugby World Cup. The reconfiguring of the rugby stadium was to swing it through 90 degrees. The title of my IWA piece was 'Zaha Hadid, Opera House or 90 degrees: A lament – perhaps not' (5 April 2016). The item attracted media interest; well at least by Radio Cymru! Later a contribution was made by the UK Millennium development project for the creation of the Millennium Centre on the site of the original plan of the *opera* house. The Millennium Centre is now the home of the Wales National Opera and is also a concert hall. Within a couple of years Wales had two prestigious centres in Cardiff, each with *Millennium* in the names within a mile of each other: The Millennium Centre and the reconfigured rugby stadium known as The Millennium Stadium. Wales is the language of song, but not opera. It was only Cardiff taxi drivers that knew the distinction between each Millennium building: the Millennium Centre, the Millennium Stadium! Wales is not only the language of song, but farce also at times.

A while later the Welsh Rugby Union needed sponsorship for financial reasons. The Principality Building Society came to the rescue in 2015 with a 10-year contract. The Stadium was *creatively* renamed the Principality Stadium. With the Principality sponsorship ending in 2025, the WRU has started searching for a new sponsor with deep pockets. At the time of writing (May 2023) with just 2 years until the end of the Principality contract a company with such very deep pockets is being sought. The supermarket Lidl? From 2025 onwards the hot money is on the Stadium being renamed the Lidl Stadium.

In my last contribution to the IWA (10 May 2018) I gave reasons for changing my mind on the European Union membership referendum - Brexit - from *remaining* in the EU to *leaving*. The title of the article was, '*Leave*: a rich democracy. *Remain*: a rich economy. Choose your risk.' The following day the IWA published a reply by the former Chair of the IWA and Wales for Europe, *in friendship*. That his immediate response to my article was published the next day might be seen as a case of *pulling power, tugged* by the, seeming, docility of the IWA. If considered suitable for publication, articles submitted to the independent IWA will usually appear a while later, not the following day. I had earlier written three IWA articles on the EU referendum.

***

My son lived first in Sydney before moving to Brisbane with his family. Sydney can be a bit chilly in the winter, so I needed to buy a winter gilet. With my son I shopped for one. We found a gilet at a reasonable price, of good quality, and we both liked it. It was in a quality county shop, selling a wide range of clothes for outdoor wear. Before buying it, I needed to try it on. The orderly pile of gilets had the highest price on top of the pile, so I went down through the pile until I found the cheapest. Unbeknown to me, the cheapest was the smallest. It was a little tight, but I kept on struggling because of the price, and my son agreed. Then as I took it off, I saw a shop assistant hiding his laughter. My son stepped back, not wanting to be associated with what I was doing. Seeing what I had been trying on he said with embarrassment, 'Dad, there are four armholes in it'. I'd been trying on a dog coat. The shop assistant approached me with the remark, 'Can I help you, sir?'. By this time the shop assistant had struggled to remain respectful. We left the store with our *tails between our legs,* so to speak, and looked elsewhere. I returned to the UK without a gilet.

Our visit to Australia was our first long haul flight. We went with Olympic Airlines. Our choice of airline was based on the lowest ticket price. Had it been safety, it would have been another airline. I learned from a Greek colleague that BA engineers maintained Olympic Airlines. The reason given by my Greek colleague was that Greek engineers could not be relied on to maintain their aircraft! Three other issues failed to give us confidence on the return flight. The aircraft was an old Boeing 747 with our seats in the upstairs bubble. Here we could look directly into the cockpit. The pilot was grossly overweight and chain-smoking. His size would give him early retirement had he been a BA pilot. To obscure the sun, newspapers were taped to the top of the windscreen. Take off was delayed as we had to wait for food to be delivered; and being close to the cockpit we could see and hear the pilot getting increasingly agitated. We changed planes in Athens and returned to London on a mid-range aircraft. We sat on the plane for ages with the cabin crew desperately trying to squeeze all passengers into the cabin. It became evident that there were more passengers than there were seats. Solution. Place overspill passengers out of sight on the floor of the galley. Problem solved. We landed. Other flights to Australia over several years were uneventful. Flatbeds were introduced, and painfully long journeys became tolerable.

Gossip has always interested me. Rather innocently, I thought that the tone of gossip would be less flippant, and less maligned, as I moved away from the workshop floor to professional jobs. Not so. The gossip just became more subtle and shrouded in the fog of policy differences. A good friend who was an English teacher once told me that unmalicious gossip oils the wheels of sanity.

Frequently I would have meetings in the Welsh Office while at FEU. Now it's probably true that gossip is mainly exchanged between people of the same status in an institution, but I was told of a short exchange between a senior civil servant and the Secretary of State for

Wales. Both had Peter as their first name. The Secretary of State wanted the relationship to be less formal. So, he broached the subject with Peter. 'Peter, I'd like you to call me Peter'. Peter replied, 'No, Secretary of State. I prefer Secretary of State', Peter, not Peter, Secretary of State.

As a child, I pestered my parents for a dog; we already had a black cat. My parents yielded, and a Welsh terrier was there when I returned home from school. I named him Ricky, which was not a very Welsh name for a Welsh black and tan terrier. The pleasure of having a dog was short-lived. He was hit by a car outside our house and his back was broken. We really should have put him down, but I had waited such a long time for a dog that I made a trolley for his legs. It didn't work because his rear legs were dragging on the ground. I bound his legs with wool, but it didn't last.

When I had children of my own it was my turn to yield, and we had an English springer spaniel from a friend's litter. We called him Sam, a novel name for an English springer. He was instantly nasty. I would take him for a mountain walk, where he frequently disappeared chasing sheep, birds and any creature within sight. We reasoned that if we had another dog, Sam might calm down. And that we did, we had a Welsh springer spaniel, Taffy, from the Rhondda valley. He was a delight, but not in Sam's eyes. He played hell with Taffy.

Sundays can be terrible, especially when low clouds and drizzle set in. One Sunday in such weather I returned from a conference to find that Sam had destroyed the new cushion floor we had just laid. We didn't have much money at the time, and the cushion floor was a statement that we were doing well, financially. That same Sunday I took the two dogs for a walk. Taffy was walking behind as usual, and Sam was nowhere to be seen. Then I heard a gunshot. A dream comes true. Sam was no more. I got home to a phone call from the farmer, to whom I apologised. Taffy lived on as a dearly loved pet until he died when the children were in their teens. We were all so upset.

Now living in Wenvoe, my wife said out of the blue, 'Let's have a dog'. I've since learned that we had Mali because of my cyclothymia condition. It helped! Her front is a schnauzer, but we are not sure about the rest of her. The vet thinks her back might be another terrier of sorts. We will never know. The farmer from where we had Mali said she was crossed with a King Charles. You'd look long and hard to find a King Charles in her. Our view is that Mali's mother was a naughty girl. Her mother was a pure miniature schnauzer. Walking Mali every day has changed our lives and she is loved by all. And most importantly my Welsh continues to improve with my 'Teach Your Dog Welsh' book.

Our nearest grandchildren we see often with their mother. Because of her expertise in the Welsh language, the children's grandmother, my wife, is on hand to help them with their schoolwork. Our grandchildren in Merthyr we see about every six-weeks. Our grandchild in East London we see a few times a year, but daily through Zoom. Our grandchildren in Brisbane we might see every two years or so, though we have frequent Zoom meetings.

18: Time to add up

I am not

I am not young enough to know everything

Oscar Wilde

Things I am proud of:

My son writing to me when he returned to Australia that he will forever be grateful for the help I gave him with his MBA, moved me powerfully.

That I took the risk of temporary employment by returning to Merthyr for marriage and taking a temporary teaching post at Merthyr Tydfil college. It was not the only time I had taken a temporary teaching job. I did the same when I returned from secondment to the Government's Further Education Unit to Cardiff University. A five-year annual rolling contract ended when I became Vice-Principal of Pontypridd College. While temporary employment contracts are a risk to one's financial income, I would never have progressed my career from an apprentice motor mechanic to senior management in the further education sector had I not taken the risk of temporary jobs.

Being invited to become a governor of a Welsh-medium school and subsequently chair of the board of governors.

Being nominated to become chair of the Valleys Initiative for Adult Education (VIAE). At the time VIAE was an ambitious high profile political initiative.

Helping our two children to gain degrees and make their way in life.

Having made a significant contribution to the development of quality in further education in Wales.

Supporting colleagues in establishing a highly successful basic skills provision for students on vocational education courses. About one third of vocational students have low levels of literacy and numeracy.

135

Being invited to be an assessor of the Beacon Awards and the Queen's Awards.

Gaining a first-class honours degree in education, and later a Masters degree in education.

Things I would do if I could turn the clock back:

I would spend much more time with my two children as they were growing up.

During my four years working at Rolls Royce in London, I would live in shared rented accommodation with friends, rather than, as I did, live in digs.

When living in London I would not return to Merthyr so often.

My Brisbane friend was 'doing' Europe. It was he who wanted me to go to Israel to live in a kibbutz for a while. Not going to Israel is one of the greatest regrets in my life. My friend returned after a year to Rolls Royce; our friendship continues to this day.

Persevere in learning Welsh.

***

My apprenticeship period was enjoyable and fundamental to my career and personal choices later in life. Being a skilled motor mechanic enabled me to work at Merthyr bus garage, and gain experience of working on heavy vehicles. However, not enjoying my time there convinced me that I should take the risk of living in London and accept that my life lay elsewhere.

The more senior I became in my education career the more I was plagued with imposter syndrome. Every time I walked into Cardiff University as a lecturer, I felt a frisson of imposter syndrome. I suppose anxiety is close to my default emotion.

My life has been fulfilling and getting over earlier adversity helped me to cope with difficult periods. My empathy for others is reinforced, knowing that I too have dealt with disappointment. I failed to be appointed as Principal in the college where I was Vice-Principal. I was disappointed but turned up to college the following day and got on with my work.

I have strived always to be rational, as my father did, though inevitably I did not always succeed, which may have led me to be impossibly intransigent on issues that were not particularly important.

As Vice-Principal, my office door was open most of the time. Colleagues did not take this as an open invitation to come in for a chat. Most would come in to make a case on some issue; then we would talk about it and often take it to the next stage of consideration. Such an approach is not prevarication; it is striving to make a sound decision with colleagues.

I'm proud that I never sought or exercised power; I have though, exercised considerable influence while Vice-Principal.

Being obsessed with my career in education was thrilling, yet now I see that it deprived me of spheres of stimulation and experiences that were lost to me. Listening to some of our new friends I see starkly the narrowness of my life, though owing to my disposition it could not have been any other way.

I have never been a member of a political party. The nearest I got to any organisation that had similar purposes as political parties, which is to influence change in the public domain and society generally, was the IWA. Educating, which I did for twenty-nine years, is the means I took of contributing to societal change. Being actively involved in trade unions is another means I took to contributing to societal change. I still enjoy party politics, government, and public and general affairs.

There have been several people who have influenced me during my education career. All were hard working, had a strong vocation regarding the purpose of further education, had integrity, and a form of leadership that gave me considerable scope to have a de facto liberal job description.

I began this memoir by mentioning several significant influences on my life.

- My early family life and sense of being enmeshed by that family.
- The Aberfan disaster
- Gaining a first-class bachelor's degree.
- Moving to London and working at Rolls Royce.
- The mental health condition cyclothymia.

These influences shaped my choice of friends, my approach to parenting with my wife, my two careers, my divorce, my second marriage, and life in retirement. I've made good and poor choices throughout life. I know not how but I have eventually overcome the poor choices. Luck maybe, determination maybe. At seventy-eight I'm content, though achieving this state of contentment was something I avoided until retirement. I considered contentment a condition without drive. It is not. It is the other side of a coin, called happiness. That is where I am today.

Epilogue

I am sure everyone has learned about the Aberfan disaster, perhaps from school or for some readers, from a mother or a father. The tragedy happened when a coal tip slipped onto the primary school which I had attended as a child. 116 children and 28 adults were buried alive on 21 October 1966. News of the tragedy spread quickly around the world.

I was 22 and living in Aberfan at the time of the disaster. Eleven months later, I moved to work in London. I am not entirely sure why I left Aberfan for London and stayed there for four years, but I think it had something to do with the profound impact that the disaster had on me then, accompanied by an ever-present scepticism about authority.

It is rare for me to say that I'm from Aberfan; I usually say I'm from Merthyr. I will seldom contribute to conversation if the disaster is mentioned. I am disturbed to this day. I am not able to settle my emotions.

I first wrote a poem shortly after the disaster when memories were fresh in my soul. Some 51 years later I felt compelled to return to the poem and convey the emotions I feel today and share those emotions. I weep inside. The following poem is how I thought about life at the age of seventy-one. It is written for my dear grandchildren with all love from their Grampy.

YESTERDAY IS TODAY

I thought I survived Aberfan. Oh no!
My valley was green
Beauty to be seen
So pleasant
Changed present
Instantly blacked
Future wracked
The people grey
Some didn't stay
To be forlorn
To be alone
To seek
Not speak
Strangling past
Present cast
Future pain
Lasting strain
It is over
It is not over
It drives ambition
It drives sedition
Peace may yet come
Peace might have come
So will the end

Now six years later I have written another poem.

Towards the end

My village changed at 9.15 or there about.
But no 'there about' with one hundred and forty-four dead.
Black tip.
Black slurry.
I moved away.
I moved back.
My heart forever somewhere in between.
My heart indelibly confused.
Young heart confused.
Old heart confused.
My lonely heart.
My lonely heart too confused to share.
My heart forever lonely.
My heart forever in turmoil.
My heart will not rest.
Maybe I should share my heart.
What should I share in my heart?
Might it be trust?
No.
The alchemy of trust turned the black tip to black slurry.
Might it be faith in Authority?
No.
It was faith in Authority that changed Aberfan to tragedy.
The dead are long rested.
I am slowly resting through shared happiness and
contentment.

Brenig Davies

Acknowledgements

I am grateful to my good friend Steve John for his encouragement as I embarked on the task of writing this memoir and his continuing support to the final copy. I had initially intended it to be read principally by my grandchildren but as I reflected on my experiences it occurred to me that it might be of wider interest. My gratitude goes to Chris Jones of Cambria Publishing for encouraging me.